Minimalism

Minimalism

History
Fashion
Design
Architecture
Interiors

h.f.ullmann

Author: Arco Editorial S.A. Barcelona

Editorial project coordinator:

Loft Publications, s.l.
Domènech 7-9, 2° 2ª
08012 Barcelona, Spain
Tel: + 34 93 218 30 99
Fax: + 34 93 237 00 60
e-mail: loft@loftpublications.com
www.loftpublications.com

Editor: Sofía Cheviakoff

Layout and typesetting: Mireia Casanovas Soley, Jaume Martínez Coscojuela, Emma Termes Parera

Text: Sofía Cheviakoff, Aurora Cuita (Epilogo), Pilar Bonet (Minimalismo-Minimalista. Una reflexión histórica.), Pablo Soto (Moda)

Text editing: Susana González Torras

Original title: Minimalismo-Minimalista. Una reflexión histórica.
ISBN: 978-3-8331-2574-4

© 2006/2007 for the English edition: Tandem Verlag GmbH
h.f.ullmann is an imprint of Tandem Verlag GmbH

Translation from Spanish: Translate-A-Book, Oxford, UK

Typesetting: Organ Graphic, Abingdon, UK

Printed in China

ISBN: 978-3-8331-4637-4

10 9 8 7 6 5 4 3 2 1
X IX VIII VII VI V IV III II I

less is more

"The canvas is never empty"

Gilles Deleuze

Minimalism: Introduction

This book looks at all the disciplines influenced by the minimalism movement. It explains what minimal art is, how it developed in 1960s New York, and how a creative sensibility, which has lasted for 40 years, was developed. This sensibility has coexisted with a number of styles and fashions, which sometimes conflicted with its principles of expressing as much as possible with as little as possible.

The book is divided into two sections: Minimalism and Minimalist. The first section looks at minimalism in terms of the creative method that slowly spread to various different art-related disciplines over the decades. We should look upon it as a new sensibility, a new system of creation arising from "minimal art" and based on a number of modernist ideals. The second section is a showcase for many of the works based on these principles. We have picked four disciplines on which the minimalist trend has had a major influence. Clearly they are not the only ones in which minimalism finds an echo; works that reflect these creative methods have been produced in music, theater, cinema, and many other areas of the performing arts.

The work of ballet dancers and choreographers, like Merce Cunningham or the German Gerhard Bohner, is directly related to minimalism. Cesc Gilabert performs Bohner's "Im (Goldenen) Schnitt II" ["Through the (golden) section"] on a completely empty white stage, with only five steel pipe sculptures by Robert Schad. The ballet dancer is dressed simply in black trousers and shirt. His ballet shoes are also black. He performs precise movements, which follow one another mechanically. On stage there's only him, the sculptures, and Heidrum Holtman playing a piano piece by Bach. Interest is focused entirely on his movements. There are no items of clothing, make-up, lighting, or scenery that might be distracting.

The works we have chosen may not all be labeled as minimalist, but they reflect this sensibility, which has gained followers in the fields of fashion, object design, furniture design, interior decorating, and, of course, architecture.

Minimal art

Minimal art appeared in New York in the 1960s, and permeated various areas of the creative arts such as sculpture, painting, dance, music, theater, film, and even fashion, in a way that was much closer to the consumer.

During this time Marilyn Monroe commits suicide and Philip Johnson declares that the Seagram Building is the last icon of modernity. The Pan Am skyscraper, designed by Walter Gropius, is built next to Grand Central Station in New York, radically transforming the urban and architectural scale of Park Avenue, one of the city's most emblematic thoroughfares. Also, Frank Lloyd Wright builds the Guggenheim next to Central Park.

Minimal art was born as the modernist period came to a close, in a society experiencing an economic boom and a profound moral crisis. Springing from the European figurative avant-garde movements like abstract expressionism, cubism, and dadaism, minimal art goes further in the search for abstraction, divesting the work of any sentiment and meaning. What is important is not the work of art, but the literature it generates around it. Minimal art shares with pop art a number of characteristics, like the idea of working in series, the reduction of plastic resources, and the display of banal or everyday objects as works of art. Andy Warhol himself filmed a video of a man sleeping for hours, with this being the only image. Carl Andre presented his rows of horizontal bricks: a simple ordering of fireproof bricks aligned on the floor. The works are cold and impersonal; the artist's role is that of an intellectual manager. "It is fundamental for me not to get my hands dirty. I reclaim art as thought." (Don Flavin)

Minimalism in architecture

Even though minimal art sprung from the crisis in modernity, a number of masters of modernity, such as Mies van der Rohe, have undeniably contributed to the development of minimalism in architecture. His famous saying, "less is more," defines minimalism as the fruit of sculptural and aesthetic reduction. The minimalist search is guided by the principle that reducing is the clearest gesture. It is no longer necessary to make the structure visible. Le Corbusier pursued purity: pure, flat, and white surfaces are more important than truth to materials or the display of the structure. Even though functionalism was a way of escaping and shedding the weight of tradition, some aspects of modernity, like the fact that it was an international style that did away with the local nature of a dwelling (such as its topography, climate, and the sociocultural features of its inhabitants), triggered a major crisis. Once modernity was over, its effects continued to be felt in the creative methods of many architects.

Sofía Cheviakoff

Minimalism

A Historical Reflection

Minimalism: A Historical Reflection

In New York in the 1960s, the United States of America had established its supremacy in the art world. This was thanks to the spread of abstract expressionism and, subsequently, of both pop art and so-called minimal art, which rejected the customary practices of pictorial composition and attempted to supplant the European artistic tradition. Culture in the great metropolis was now manufacturing its own modernity, and challenging the conditions and limits of the modernist movement.

New trends in art and architecture had demonstrated that traditional artistic categories were no longer viable, and had shown an urgent need to establish new relations between theory and practice, which would value the importance of the viewer's perception. After 1945, which is generally considered to be the dividing line between the development of the artistic avant-garde and the successive proliferation of post-avant-garde trends, Paris lost its artistic pre-eminence and the American model imposed itself on Europe. As a demonstration of this change of direction, the Venice Biennale of 1964 awarded its first prize to the pop artist Robert Rauschenberg. Any future discussion about art would be a discussion about international art. North American art had enriched Western culture with its

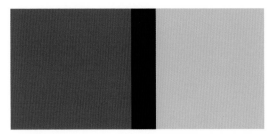

Barnett Newman, *Who's afraid of red, yellow, and blue?*, 1969–1970, oil on canvas.

Andy Warhol, *Four Marilyns*, 1962, polymer and silk-screen printing on canvas.

freedom from the burdens of the avant-garde movement, which had always been a contradictory and dogmatic modernity.

The 1960s also witnessed the confirmation of the United States as the wealthiest and most powerful nation on earth. The peculiar structure of American society, with its social organization, its strong sense of pragmatism, its consumer-oriented market system, and its fast pace, would thereafter set the standards of conduct for Western art. However, despite the appearance of more radical artistic creations after 1945, and especially during the 1970s, there was no evidence of a

Frank Stella, *Ouray*, 1961, copper paint on canvas.

definitive break with the historical avant-garde of the inter-war period. Abstract expressionist painters were inspired by European surrealism, and reinvented abstraction. Minimalist artists, like Donald Judd, demonstrated the feasibility of adopting constructivism and dadaist objectuality in his "specific objects," just as Louis Kahn's architecture broke away from the axioms of Mies van der Rohe and developed the new, striking personality of American architecture.

Mies van der Rohe, Seagram Building, 1954–1958. New York.

American art in the 1960s confirmed that, in their cultural context, styles developed 30 years earlier had a specific path of development. The time for assimilation had passed, and the avant-garde movement, which culminated in Europe between 1920 and 1940, had become a crucial element of new theoretical models that rejected its utopian vision but pursued its explorations. In the 1960s art showed how the established view of things was in crisis. In this critical context, the spirit of minimalism, with its aesthetic search for simple shapes and clear structures, became one of the major catalysts for the conception and development of the principal artistic and architectural periods of the following decades.

From the mid-1970s onward, minimalist theory stimulated the development of an unprecedented relationship between the work of art and the viewer, in terms of perception mechanisms, a relationship that explored the modern tradition and its boundaries. Each artistic and architectural contribution gave rise to an examination of its materiality and the possibility of dematerialization. The European works of Wassily Kandinsky, Kazimir Malevich, or Piet Mondrian, like the designs of Walter Gropius, Mies van der Rohe, or Le Corbusier, were seminal in this search for a new artistic quality. This is because, like the literature of James Joyce, the music of Arnold Schönberg, or the philosophy of Ludwig Wittgenstein, they reveal the purely structural, formal, compositional, and conceptual aspects of the new art.

The methods of the European avant-garde and the aesthetics of modernity in architecture influenced the character and urban landscape of New York. The rigid, reductionist style of Mies van der Rohe became the predominant architectural style. The Seagram Building on Park Avenue (1954–1958), which he

Frank Lloyd Wright, Guggenheim Museum, 1956–1959. New York.

designed with Philip Johnson, is, with its monochrome facade, undoubtedly the last great piece of modern architecture. At the same time, it marks a turning point for Modernism. Many architects specialized in imitating its style, but others turned away from the so-called international style[1] and tried out other methods of construction. These ranged between wild design and the somewhat less irrational, the rediscovery of modern classicism, and the opportunity to conceive buildings as sculptures. Frank Lloyd Wright's revolutionary spiral-shaped Guggenheim Museum in New York (1956–1959), a symbol of popular culture in a modern artistic form, set a new standard.

Over the past 30 years, art and architecture have been characterized by a pervasive desire for exploration, which has opened up many, occasionally divergent, routes. The book by the American architect Robert Venturi entitled *Complexity and Contradiction in Architecture* (1966), published at the same time as pop art was in ascendancy and minimal art was in its infancy in the United States, is a clear demonstration of a burgeoning post-modern sensitivity. It promotes architectural design that makes use of seemingly disparate elements, a complex and contradictory, inclusive, conventional, and eclectic type of architecture, which is also full of tension, ambiguities, and transgressions. Venturi's own architecture recreated the compositional principles of the most restrictive type of classicism, introducing additional elements borrowed from the pop art repertoire.

[1] The term "international style" was first coined in 1932 at the exhibition of modern architecture in the New York Museum of Modern Art. The historian Henry Russell Hitchcock and the architect Philip Johnson were the promoters of this exhibition, which polarized the aesthetics of architectural modernity.

Roy Lichtenstein, *Eddie Diptych*, 1962, oil on canvas.

In the mid-1960s a series of circumstances fostered the development of minimal art, a kind of art which, if we understand history to be a succession of revolutions, can only be considered counter-revolutionary. Coming between conceptual art and pop art, the role of minimalism, with its reductionist language, is not purely and strictly to revise avant-garde modernity but to move beyond art, to an artistic fusion.[2] Despite their diversity, minimalist works display a number of common features: total abstraction, maximum order, neutrality and anti-illusionism, use of elementary shapes (sometimes presented as a series of modular systems), minimum complexity, and use of industrial materials. Is this a new nihilism, or new art?[3]

As New York replaced Paris as art capital of the world, Allan Kaprow was making sure that the people attending his "happenings" were co-authors, and Andy Warhol was dissolving the boundaries between the concepts of high and low culture. A number of artists were starting a similar revolution. This was based on the minimalist purity of the naked form, oscillating between the sculptural introversion of geometry and its expanded use in architecture. Their aim was to create works that were specific and completely independent objects, rejecting traditional pictorial and sculptural concepts. The blunt, elementary shapes of this minimalist art strongly influenced ideas about the essence of art and the role of the spectator. In the culture of the 20th century there was a return to sobriety, a rejection of ornamentation, and a new search for the essence of geometry. It was an artistic trend that Michael Fried called "literalism" in his definition of the extremely strong, dominant, and unitary shapes

[2] For an analysis of the direction and continuity of minimalism and of its attempt to transform radically the concept of a work of art and the artist's role, see Kenneth Baker's book, *Minimalism, Art of Circumstance*. Abbeville Press, New York, 1988.

[3] Terms used by the minimalist Donald Judd in an interview for *Art News* in September 1966.

of minimalism, which had already been apparent in the "field paintings" of Ad Reinhardt, Barnett Newman, and Frank Stella, but were now becoming widespread.

Minimalism should be seen as a timeless and inter-disciplinary category, characterized by a desire for functional and conceptual simplicity and able to apply new aesthetic strategies to art and architecture. As a new movement, minimalism in art integrates the abstractionist currents of the avant-garde with the phenomenological thinking of Merleau-Ponty. Minimalism in this decade went to great pains to express the carnal presence of the elementary in its perceptive evidence, imposing itself on the viewer with the authority of what is evident.[4] Without any doubt, its essence set the standards for the future development of art, and was the basis for all discussion about art at the end of the last century.

The most significant works and artists of the last few decades have used minimalism as a critical medium to confront art with its new role in society, in the non-representational, self-referential framework provided by minimal art.

[4] Maurice Merleau-Ponty, *Phenomenology of Perception* (1945). Peninsula. Barcelona, 1975.

Minimal Art

The term "minimalism" was first coined in an article published by the critic Richard Wollheim in the journal *Arts Magazine* in January 1965. Entitled "Minimal Art," the article discussed dadaism and neodadaism and examined one of the features of modern aesthetics: the desire to dissolve content in the pictorial sense of the term. In his examination, the critic made no distinction between works of pop art, such as those created by Andy Warhol or Roy Lichtenstein, with their methods of appropriating prefabricated icons, and industrial pieces produced by artists such as Robert Morris and Donald Judd. Wollheim, a professor of philosophy at University College London, believed that both practices had the same purpose: to minimize the artistic content of the finished product. According to Wollheim, if we look at how the contemporary art scene has developed over the past 50 years, we can see an increasing acceptance of objects that, although dissimilar in appearance, purpose, and moral impact, have a common characteristic or feature: they share a minimalist artistic content. This may be because they are impossible to differentiate from one another and, therefore, have a minimum content of some kind. Alternatively, it may be because the obvious difference between them, which in some cases can be considerable, comes not from the artist but from a non-artistic source, such as nature or the factory.[5]

[5] Richard Wollheim, "Minimal Art", *Arts Magazine*, 1965, text included in Gregory Battcock's publication *Minimal Art: A Critical Anthology*, E.P. Dutton, New York, 1968; University of California Press, 1995.

Robert Morris, installation in the Green Gallery, 1964, New York.

Despite the criticism and controversy that minimalist works provoked, and the different terms used to designate a new situation in art at the end of the 1960s, the term minimalism has since been adopted to define the reductionist sculptures of American artists Carl Andre, Donald Judd, Dan Flavin, Sol LeWitt, and Robert Morris, among others. It has also been used as a label to describe common approaches in the field of architecture, design, music, or dance when they are in keeping with the modern tradition of expressing, or displaying, the elementary with the greatest economy of means of expression. The term minimalism, therefore, connects with the principle of construction in its most ascetic versions and with the gestalt devices of the psychology of form.

During their first joint exhibition in 1966, at the Jewish Museum of New York, the artists themselves defined the works displayed in etymological terms, as "primary structures." In any case, the term minimal or minimalist – which replaces names such as cool art, nihilist art, serial art, or even idiot art – has become the key word to describe a major trend in contemporary art, architecture, and thinking. Minimalism is characterized by practices that spurn narrative and iconographic intention and find self-referential fulfillment in simple geometry, in the austerity of emptiness and in the directness of the present. The objects used have the ability to say nothing and to possess no internal organization of shapes or signals.

Andy Warhol, *White Brillo Boxes*, 1964, silk-screen print on wood.

In the words of Donald Judd, minimal art creations define and describe "new work" and essentially alter the meaning of form from its traditional value to one that is continuously evolving. "Painting and sculpture have become established forms. Much of their significance has no credibility. The use of three dimensions is not the use of a specific shape. Too few works have been created and too little time has passed for us to perceive their limits. To date, the three dimensions in their widest sense are, first and foremost, a space within which we can evolve..."[6]

For Richard Wollheim, who has examined the origins of this minimalist condition, the tactics of Ad Reinhardt's black paintings, with no visible traces of any gesture, are comparable to Marcel Duchamp's unassisted ready-mades. Duchamp took simple industrial objects out of their context and displayed them as works of art without any intermediate handling by the artist. This coexistence between the elementary forms of the avant-garde tradition of abstract painting and Duchamp's object principle may be surprising. At first sight they are paradoxical, because they contradict the hypothetical or actual purity of shape and media, but in reality they are not so because minimal art shares the theory of materiality with the more dadaist versions of pop art. Wollheim challenges the transgressive sensitivity of art in the 1960s, identifying its common structures, beginning with Duchamp's ready-made creations. In the same way – albeit with a different result – Barbara Rose examines the new art in her article "ABC Art," published in 1965. Here she likens pop art and minimal art to Duchamp and even Malevich.[7] The author makes an accurate critical contribution to the new aesthetic scenario, noting a generalized renunciation of singularity, beginning with a rejection of the unbridled pictorial

[6] Donald Judd, "Specific Objects", in *Arts Yearbook*, no. 8, 1965, pages 74–82.
[7] Barbara Rose, "ABC Art", in *Art in America*, October 1965.

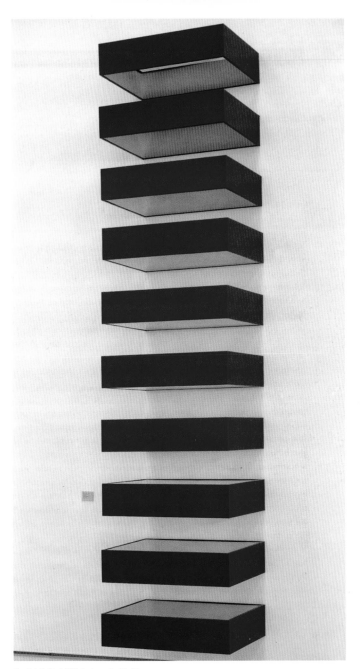

Donald Judd, *Starck*, 1990, aluminum and red Plexiglas.

subjectivity of expressionism and the re-establishment of a new complexity. This, she says, allows minimalist and pop artists to introduce other forms and content into art.

Minimal art and pop art are interconnected schisms of the 1960s, and key developments in contemporary history. They advocate two developments that are the conceptual driving forces of art and architecture in the 1980s and 1990s: the "death of the author," in the words of Roland Barthes, and the "birth of the reader," the driver of post-modernist sensitivity. The apparent simplicity of minimalism, like the redundant iconic and media piracy of pop art, deliberately opens up a gap between what is and what is not art, appropriating Wittgenstein's tenets, according to which things (objects) are just literal and emphatic statements of their existence.

Barbara Rose was one of the first critics to deal with the phenomenon of the minimal condition among artists of the 1960s. According to Rose, a new sensitivity had developed, but what it consisted of was as yet unclear.[8] Dan Flavin's neons, Donald Judd's metal plates or Richard Serra's steel are existing, prefabricated materials. Like the icons of the consumer society used by pop artists — soup cans, Coca-Cola bottles, and cinema legends, for example — they attempt to achieve a kind of new objectivity by their existence as objects. For the artists of the 1960s, this sublimation of the world of objects is a philosophical condition, a critical condition.

In Barbara Rose's view, the concept of minimal art could be applied to the empty, repetitive, and rigid art of many painters, sculptors, ballet dancers, and composers of the time. This description did not, however, imply that the concept had been

[8] Barbara Rose, op.cit. page 33.

Richard Serra, *Olson*, 1985–1986.

Robert Rauschenberg, *Coca-Cola Plan*, 1958, The Museum of Contemporary Art, Los Angeles. The Panza Collection.

interpreted in a negative way, as Professor Wollheim pointed out, but that a path of discovery had been followed which drove art to resist interpretation. This is the real and fundamental distinguishing feature of art of the 1960s. As Barbara Rose says, the work describes itself but does not interpret itself, and statements about its content, meaning, or intention are important only because they are omitted.[9] This omission undoubtedly troubles the viewer, and triggers a new aesthetic experience that creates a novel and renovative relationship between form and content, object and viewer, parameters that establish the coordinates of contemporary art. Even though you may be standing in front of something that is nothing, you feel something, and normally something that troubles you quite a bit. Perhaps what you feel is that, contrary to the extravagant and decorative fullness of the tormented previous generation, the hollowness and nudity of the emptiness has a certain moving and possibly overwhelming power of expression.[10]

According to Barbara Rose, the reserved impersonality of minimalist works and their rejection of any subjectivism are antidotes to the excessive rationality and commercialization of art. This is because they question the usefulness of art as a seductive and fanciful consumer good, its ambiguous function in our consumer culture. Rose feels that, since it is the most elusive and ambivalent kind of art, minimal art is just as difficult to talk about as it is to own.

Challenging the programmatic ideas contained in the writings of minimal artists, the critic Michael Fried, in his article "Art and Objecthood" (1967), revised the reductionist perspective of minimal art, accusing it of theatricality because of its excessive

[9] Barbara Rose, op.cit. page 38.
[10] Barbara Rose, op.cit. page 38.

literalism. Fried stated that minimal art is just as literal as any other art it tries to deny, and that its apparent emptiness is just a way of hiding its anthropomorphism because it draws the viewer into its biomorphic concealment. You just have to walk into the room where the literalist work has been placed to become a viewer, a one-person audience, as if the work in question had been waiting for you. This is because literalist works require the presence of the viewer: they are incomplete without one, they have been waiting for one...

Formed in the maelstrom of critical review that characterized the 1960s, minimal artists are today among the most important artists of the second half of the 20th century. Their work, now over 30 years old, displayed the modernizing energy that had characterized the early 20th century, which forged the minimalist challenge to the order of modern aesthetics. "At first sight everything appears simple: the specificity of Judd's Plexiglas, the presence of Morris's polyhedrons, the immediacy of Serra's iron flagstones, the logic of LeWitt's lattices, the self-reference of Bell's crystal cubes, etc. However, in each case there is a subtle ambiguity that complicates things... Even though it may be difficult to re-experience the surprise of the minimalist experience, its intellectual surprise remains, because minimalism breaks with the formal space of modern sculpture..."[11]

[11] Hal Foster, "The Essence of Minimalism," in *Minimal Art*, text included in Gregory Battcock's publication *Minimal Art: A Critical Anthology*, E.P. Dutton, New York, 1968; University of California Press, 1995.

Robert Morris, *Nine Fiberglass Sleeves*, 1967, fiberglass.

Robert Morris

Robert Morris is one of the most emblematic artists of the minimal art movement. His work, which spans a period of over 30 years, is diverse and surprising. His dedication to music (he collaborated with La Monte Young), his practice of "performances" (in 1961 he took part in the first "happenings" in New York and worked with Carolee Schneemann), his relationship with dance (as a ballet dancer and choreographer with Ann Halprin, Simone Fort, and Yvonne Rainer), his important contributions to theory (his 1966 "Notes on Sculpture" confirmed his standing as a critic), and his work with nature make Morris one of the principal theorists of minimal art and one of the most inventive North American artists.

Born in 1931 in Kansas City, Robert Morris studied engineering and history of art during the 1950s. In 1957 and 1958 he exhibited his paintings in a San Francisco gallery, and in 1968 he settled in New York. Here he quickly joined avant-garde circles and used his work to display the principles of minimalism: concern for the visual perception of the viewer, and the relationship between works of art and the spaces that contain them. In 1964, he presented structures at New York's Green Gallery, which he called unitary shapes and which introduced a new relationship between the work and the viewer, the work and the gallery space, and also the work and the issue of artistic commodities.[12]

Robert Morris is the only minimal artist to have made kinetic perception and corporal response the central aspects of his work. He generally chooses shapes to provoke kinetic reactions and convey feelings to the viewer that confirm his/her physical

[12] See Michael Craig-Martin's essay published in the catalog *Minimalism* by Tate Gallery Liverpool, Liverpool, 1989, on the importance of the viewer's role.

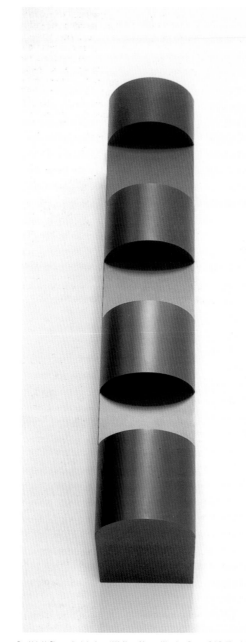

Donald Judd, *Blue anodized aluminum*, 1973, Neues Museum Weserburg Bremen. Col. Dr. Klaus Lafrenz.

presence in the same space as the object. At the Green Gallery exhibition, the bluntness and clarity of his pieces focused attention on six different areas of the hall. Visitors entering the exhibition had to walk under one of the objects and then found themselves surrounded by all the others. By being forced to move around the three-dimensional shapes, viewers took possession of them, turning from viewers into *performers*.

According to Morris, art is a situation in which you react to part of your awareness of art. This definition is in line with Marcel Duchamp's ideas. Together with Donald Judd, Morris has contributed the most to defining the problems inherent in minimalist practice, such as the rejection of any sensual contamination by the history of art.[13]

Morris believes that movement is fundamental; therefore cutting pieces of felt (1967) and leaving them scattered wherever they may fall, is a way of avoiding the content of form, the strict division of figures, in favor of the radical materiality of objects. Minimalism, according to Morris, creates global, instant and gestaltic structures that are immediately assimilated by the mind of the viewer and become a non-sensual kind of art. His unitary shapes are sculptures that make it impossible to isolate elements by interpretation. Even when he introduces changeable elements, such as steam, water, or earth in his works and installations, the changing nature of the materials, the brutality of the change, and the resulting disorientation it produces in the viewer serve to explore new forms of perception.

During the 1970s, Morris worked on monumental structures in open spaces. The Observatory, a project he worked on between

[13] Robert Morris' "Notes on Sculpture" in *Artforum* magazine, New York, 1966, describe a series of problems inherent in minimal sculpture and examine the issues of scale, size, surface, and the gestaltic nature of new sculptures, as well as the issue of viewer participation.

1970 and 1977, is a circular construction with a diameter of 300 feet (91 meters), which is accessed along a narrow path. Once inside, the spectator has the feeling that he/she is both the viewer and the viewed, and feels like an object at the center of a totalitarian space. From the 1980s onward, Morris abandoned the minimalist register and explored painting with a markedly expressionist feel.

Donald Judd, *Untitled*, 1966, galvanized metal and Plexiglas.

Donald Judd

Donald Judd is one of the most radical minimalists. His works are characterized by extreme formal simplicity and the absence of ambiguity. The fact that none of his works have a title accentuates the non-referential aspect of his geometric structures, and his writings can be considered theoretical treatises on minimalism.

Born in 1928, Judd studied philosophy, and it was not until 1955 that he completed his first paintings, in which he insisted on not displaying feelings or portraying any images. In 1959 he gave up painting and concentrated on art criticism, an activity he pursued until 1965. Judd felt that art must reflect the artist's knowledge and convictions. The best art, according to Judd, demonstrates that personal decisions reflecting the artist's experience have been put into practice, and are instantly recognized by the viewer. In line with this thinking, from the beginning of the 1960s, he displayed his preference for a geometric approach to creating works of art and to the maximum possible reduction of its constitutive elements. His rectangular pictures were increasingly distilled until, in 1962, they became three-dimensional objects in various different forms, such as wall-mounted and stacked boxes, displaying his preference for the cube. Judd coined the term "specific object"[14] in order to exclude traditional pictorial and sculptural concepts. The experience of the present he wishes to create is only possible if the historical artistic tradition is not evoked, and the hierarchical relationships between the parts and any anthropomorphic intention are denied.

---

[14] Donald Judd's article "Specific Objects" in *Arts Yearbook* no. 8, 1965, values the contribution of minimalist practice as an effective reaction against the insufficiencies of traditional painting and sculpture. New specific objects convert the three dimensions into a real space.

Carl Andre, *Copper Magnesium Alloy Square*, 1969, one hundred copper and magnesium plaques. Fischer Collection. Konrad Fischer Gallery.

Judd's first personal exhibition was in New York's Green Gallery in 1963. It demonstrated that his basic concerns were the use of different materials – plastic, copper, and wood – and the presence of geometric shapes. In 1964, he produced his first wall-mounted box, which was constructed in a metalworking factory to avoid any inaccuracies in the execution. Judd displayed his first stacked construction at the Leo Castelli Gallery in 1966. His formal language was already well-defined: reduced shapes, raw materials, impersonal industrial constructions, plain colors, use of accurate mathematical progressions, and procedural pragmatism. Judd uses compact shapes and modules with uniform surfaces, which contain no references and could also be applied to his architectural projects and to his furniture. His conception of sculpture as a physical place led him to adopt an architectural approach: minimalist sculpture is conceived in relation to its environment, but not determined by it.

Unlike Carl Andre, for example, Judd retained a specific interest in color from his training as a painter, although he considered it a structure rather than a part of the artistic composition. He used one of his favorite colors, cadmium red, to define corners and contours. Both the color and the scale of his objects defined the notion of sculpture.

Sol LeWitt, *Structures N° 11*. 1986, lacquered wood. Private collection, Spain.

Carl Andre

Born in 1935 in Quincy, a coastal town south of Boston, Carl Andre maintained close artistic relations with Frank Stella between 1951 and 1953. During a journey to Europe, he visited the megalithic site of Stonehenge in England. On his return to New York, he wrote poems and songs and was introduced to the world of sculpture by Stella. He concentrated on wooden sculptures and reductionist works in the style of Brancusi. The principles of minimal art are evident in Frank Stella's early pictures. Having seen the series of flag pictures by Jasper Johns in 1958, Stella set out to eradicate the traditional and illusory pictorial space from painting in an abstract way, avoiding any reference to popular iconography. Stella's intention was therefore to demonstrate that paintings are material objects. Soon after, minimal art tackled the problem, and demonstrated concretely that there is no internal difference between the medium and the material.

In 1959, for financial reasons, Andre worked on the railroads in Pennsylvania, and the horizontality of railroad architecture led him to develop new formal ideas. That same year he exhibited one of his pyramids, *Cedar Piece*, in New York, which marked his entry into the world of contemporary sculpture. In 1965 he took part in the "Shape and Structures" exhibition, with Robert Morris, Donald Judd, and Larry Bell, at the Tibor de Nagy Gallery in New York. Months later he exhibited there on his own, in a

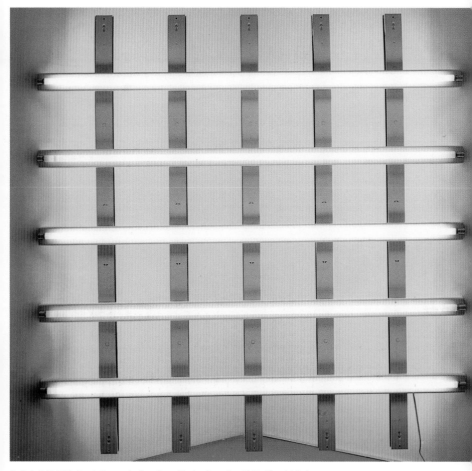

Dan Flavin, *Untitled*, 1966, pink and yellow neon tubes. Neues Museum Weserburg Bremen. Ute and Reinhard Onnasch Collection.

Dan Flavin, *Untitled*, 1966–1968, pink and yellow fluorescent tubes and daylight.

show that expressed his sculptural language and the basic concepts of his work: flatness, sculpture as a place, modular composition, and the use of inexpensive materials.

Carl Andre's great contribution is undoubtedly the way in which he liberated sculpture from its verticality, making the ascending poetry of Brancusi's endless column reversible and generating an infinite space close to the ground. In Andre's sculptures references to the body or to the traditional human figure are totally absent. All internal and external perception is removed, and the mass of the material is fully visible. All topographical references are suppressed, and all parts of the composition are of equal importance. The flatness of his works introduces a new concept and perception: sculpture is no longer an independent element; sculpture becomes a place. Carl Andre stated that he always conceived his pieces to fit the spaces in which they were to be exhibited, and that they would not exist outside these spaces. The sculpture would be tangible and visible in the same space in which the viewer had his experience by walking on the sheet metal and around the constructed area. Andre's works break many of the rules of modern sculpture. Whereas Brancusi integrated the pedestal with the sculpture, Andre suppressed it altogether and emphasized its perception in the real time of experience, in the real space: "For me, sculptures are like roads ... All my works force the viewer to walk around them, on them..."[15]

[15] Carl Andre interviewed by Phyllis Tuchman in *Artforum* magazine, New York, June 1970.

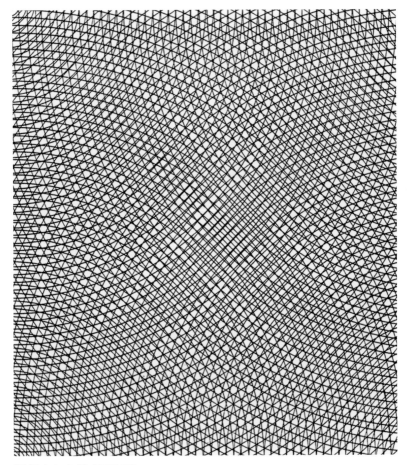

Sol LeWitt, *Arcs from Four Sides*, 1971, black pencil.

Carl Andre used standard materials repetitively – wood, lead, aluminum, stone, copper – creating extremely simple modular systems: verticality, horizontality, squares, hexagons, and crosses. He did not invent any singular shapes or any specific sculptural techniques. His method concentrated on the appreciation of materials and space rather than on the artist's gesture. His sculpture thus refuses to occupy a space, and generates its own place founded on a new spatial practice, where it is impossible to continue contemplating the work with the usual traditional models of behavior.[16]

[16] In the *Repetitive Structures* catalog, Simón Marchán Fiz examines the conceptual and operative strategies of repetition and of pure visibility as the bases for the phenomenological implication of minimal art. Fund. Juan March, Madrid, 1985.

Dan Flavin

Born in New York in 1933, Dan Flavin began his artistic training in 1952. His first works, paintings inspired by abstract expressionism, combined painting with objects. In 1961, in his first solo exhibition at the Judson Gallery, he presented paintings as elements adhering to the frame, specifically light bulbs. In 1963 he took a decisive step, fixing a white neon tube diagonally on the wall of his studio and dedicating it to Brancusi. From then on, Dan Flavin established the fundamental aspects of his work and made light his essential material. In Flavin's words, whether the light is white or colored, whether it is positioned vertically, horizontally or staggered, whether it shines from a single tube or from a composition of several pieces, on the wall or on the floor … light creates situations. It's not a question of pre-architectural or architectural structures but of places for perception.

According to Flavin, technical factors do not concern the artist; all the work is in the hands of specialists, materials come from industry, and he has no interest whatsoever in the 'do-it-yourself' approach. "My icons are concentrated constructions that celebrate naked pieces. They bring a limited amount of light…"[17] For Flavin, light generates a new dimension in pictorial experience, but only in the viewer's real time. Most of Flavin's luminous creations are untitled, but are accompanied by subtitles referring to friends, to avant-garde artists or collectors, to the place of the original installation, or to specific historical events. Examples are *Untitled (Monument for V. Tatin)*, 1975; and *Untitled (To the people of the French Revolution)*, 1987. Neon tubes arranged in simple geometric shapes, with colored fluid, are present both visually and physically, but are both diluted and encompass the entire illuminated space.

[17] Dan Flavin. *Artforum* magazine, New York, December 1967, pages 24–25.

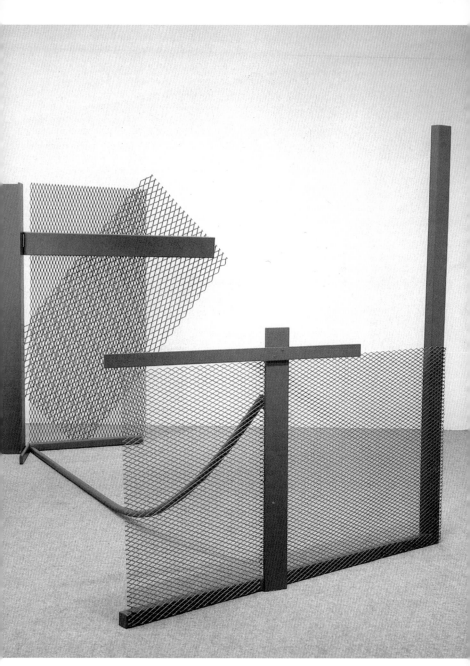

Anthony Caro, *Carriage*, 1966, painted steel.

Sol LeWitt

Sol LeWitt's work stands apart in the field of minimalism. His inclusion in minimal art has been the subject of much debate, and the artist himself rejects the term, defining his artistic work, in 1967, as conceptual art. In a famous article published in the magazine *Artforum*,[18] he defined a new kind of work, different from that of the minimalists, making critical judgements about the concepts of minimal art. In particular, LeWitt described his own approach to minimal conceptual art.

Born in 1928 in Connecticut, he practiced initially in a design school and in I.M. Pei's architectural studio. At the beginning of the 1960s he found himself in agreement with Dan Flavin, Robert Ryman, and the art critic Lucy R. Lippard, who wrote the most significant texts of the time on minimal and conceptual art. His first works, in 1962, demonstrate his knowledge of Bauhaus theories and his training as a designer. His first solo exhibition in 1965 marked the beginning of a creative period based on several fundamental principles, including: the object achieved is no more than the final, tangible product of an idea, which the author signs as the originator of the work. His structures are produced in specialized workshops in the same way as his murals are actually painted by assistants. For him, the idea or concept is the most important part of the work: the idea is the machine that produces art.

[18] Sol LeWitt, "Paragraphs on Conceptual Art," *Artforum* magazine, New York, summer 1967.

His structures, whether simple or complex, are conceived according to a rigid logic that, above all, excludes the personal factor. As systems, they serve to demonstrate both that his works are physical objects and that by merely thinking about something you have conceived it. The three-dimensional structures are white, almost always made of metal, impersonal, and devoid of any style. Sol LeWitt tends to counter the coldness and lack of emotion in his works by creating large physical structures. His aim is to remove any form of representation and expression. His structures are not formal elements but organized concepts, which demystify visual presence by using an obvious language based on simple geometrical units: lines, angles, and cubes. The proliferation of shapes in this mental and visual logic ranges between concept and object, experimenting with all the possible permutations of a given number of variations. The process could be endless and the combinations limitless. How and where is the work finished?

LeWitt's system assigns a vital role to the viewer, whose movement around the piece modifies his/her vision of the shape. When works of art are monumental in size, members of the public become actors rather than spectators. LeWitt's works are the materialization of a theoretical model devised between 1967 and 1969, which is ambivalent about its relationship with minimal art and conceptual art. Essentially, though, LeWitt's series of structures and their transparent logic are a paradigm of minimal art.

Richard Serra

Even though he may be outside the inner circle of minimalist sculptors, Richard Serra, born in San Francisco in 1939, uses steel to explore the space between American painting of the 1950s and the minimalist sculpture of the 1960s. For Serra, the physical property of the materials – rubber, lead, steel – is very important, and becomes a theme at the same time as the form is being created. The form in itself has no meaning; what is really important is the transformation that the materials undergo in opposition to any narrative purpose. His steel panel constructions, which are sited both in internal and external spaces, are produced by specialized firms working according to his instructions. They often create spaces characterized by a fragile balance: steel panels leaning against a wall, corners of a room, vast walls which section off urban spaces... The weight of the material is perceptible; the panels are not fixed and have a tense equilibrium, thanks to the force of gravity.

Richard Serra, *Afangar*, 1990.

Viewers experience these objects by Serra, occasionally produced on an architectural scale, not just visually but also physically, with their bodies. The works, as Judd suggested, can be taken in at a glance, but you immediately perceive the relation between the parts of the structure and the force acting between them. In the case of *House of Cards* (1969), the thickness of the lead panels produces the tense stability of the cube. Viewers are forced to place themselves between stability and instability. Serra's sculptures always take place in the presence of the spectator.

Even though its works are not uniform in a stylistic sense, minimal art fervor invaded the New York art world. Many exhibitions succeeded one another in galleries and museums and, although it was not a generational style, the seeds of reductionism were sown, greatly influencing aesthetic theory and achieving enormous commercial success.

British artists, particularly Anthony Caro with his sculptures, also made their specific contributions to defining the new minimalist art.

Donald Judd, *Untitled*, 1986.

The European Background: *less is more*

With the exception of a few isolationist attitudes, minimal artists and their work are indebted to the European modern tradition in the areas of neoplasticism, suprematism and constructivism, as well as Duchampian dadaism. Their projects examine the implications of the aesthetic decisions of both Malevich and Duchamp in a new context, and we could even venture to say that, thanks to their architectural quality, they achieve a culmination of this tradition by breaking through and moving beyond modern sculptural concepts.

Kazimir Malevich, *Black Square*, 1923, oil on canvas. State Russian Museum.

Kazimir Malevich, *Black Cross*, 1923, oil on canvas. State Russian Museum.

Just as pop art did in painting, minimal art led to an increase in the size of works of art in sculpture. It generated new proportions in which to develop a unitary conception of space as a structure, a "single," as Donald Judd described it, with architectural aspects. It exists on the edge of the wider field of sculpture analyzed by Rosalind Krauss in her famous essay "Sculpture in the Wider Field" (1979). This orientation of elementary geometric figures toward sculptural introversion or architectural expansion offers minimal art an intermediate field of exploration, a no-man's land where a new category is born – defined by Judd as "specific objects" – which rejects the purely visual character of modern sculpture.[19]

[19] Simón Marchán Fiz used the term "purovisibilista" to analyze the new aesthetic space introduced by minimal art in the 1960s in "La Historia del Cubo" [History of the Cube], *Minimal Art y Fenomenología* [Minimal Art and Phenomenology], Rekalde, Bilbao, 1994.

Marcel Duchamp, *Bicycle Wheel*, 1913, bicycle wheel fixed on a kitchen stool.

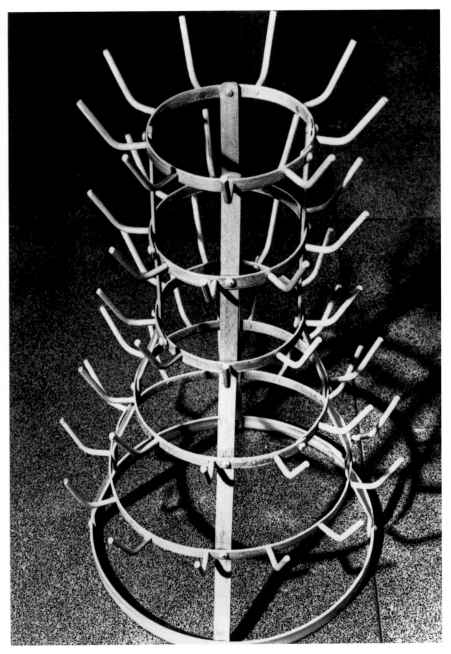

Marcel Duchamp, *Bottle Holder*, 1914, galvanized iron.

Tracing its modern itinerary, minimal art merged with the classical tradition and produced a new and abstract kind of classicism inherited from the avant-garde. This classical strain in minimalism has clear precedents, not in painting or sculpture but in architecture and in the attention paid by Le Corbusier to the presence of geometric solids in his book *Towards a New Architecture* (1923).

Recourse to elementary geometric shapes was not new in the history of art, but it was new in sculpture. Minimal art filtered the history of abstract classicism, invoking the essential principles of geometry, rejecting metaphysical order in favor of a perceptive and phenomenological experience. Minimalist works required simplicity and an economy of expressive methods, as well as aesthetic perception in the eyes of the viewer. This economy was achieved precisely by using these elementary geometric solids as defined by Plato, by employing the essential, by restricting oneself to the level zero of Malevich's suprematist painting, to Mies van der Rohe's "less is more," to *die gute Form* (good form) of German rationalist design, as well as to the structural thinking of Wittgenstein's philosophy, or Samuel Beckett's "style-free" theater.

r, Villa Savoy.

From the reductionist spirit of the avant-garde, the elementary features of Bauhaus design, and the machinist paradigm of Le Corbusier in art, architecture, and industrial and graphic design in the 20th century, there has been an exceptional journey through the world of geometric shapes and structures. This journey has avoided all allusions and illusions in favor of a blunt and self-referential language.

If the essence of 20th-century reductionism could be expressed in a few words, "less is more" would seem to summarize modern culture. This phrase, which was occasionally uttered by the taciturn Mies van der Rohe, together with *beinahe nichts* (almost nothing) actually sums up a fundamental part of the modern artistic experience. Just as classical architecture was defined by Vitruvius as *firmitas, utilitas et venustas*, part of 20th-century art and architecture could be described by Mies' operative principle: "less is more." This was the architect who designed buildings as minimalist as the

German pavilion at the universal exhibition of Barcelona (1929), as light in structure as Farnsworth House in Illinois (1949–1951), as monolithic as the Seagram Building in New York (1958), or as magnificently pure in shape as the Nationalgalerie in Berlin (1968). The very concept of less is more, its very limitation, is what achieves great mastery.

Less is more refers not to a fashion or a new trend but to a position that was reached at various times throughout the century. It represented the almost unattainable objective of causing an emotional reaction without resorting to a mass of decorative or symbolic elements, managing to express the maximum with the minimum of gestures, words, musical notes, and shapes. This search for maximum formal and conceptual tension with a restricted use of shapes or elements has been an intermittent feature of the past few decades, forging a paradoxical "maximalism": to achieve the maximum with the minimum.

Piet Mondrian, *Composition in Red, Yellow and Blue*, 1922.

The trend toward abstraction, simplification, and elementarism was one of the driving forces of the artistic and architectural avant-garde in the 20th century. Adolfo Loos, Mies van der Rohe, Hannes Meyer, and Ludwig Hilberseimer supported maximum reductionism in architecture and town planning, just as Piet Mondrian, Kazimir Malevich, Wassily Kandinsky, and Paul Klee did in painting, or Gertrude Stein, Ezra Pound, and Raymond Chandler did in literature.

As a category, less is more is not fixed in time but has continued to develop in architecture and design, as in art. The sculptural works of Tony Smith – an architect who worked with Wright in 1939 and who took up sculpture in the 1960s – as well as the luminescent interiors created by Dan Flavin or the box

Marcel Breuer, *Stahlrohrstuhl* B33, 1928.

Marcel Breuer, *Lattenstuhl*, 1922.

Laszlo Moholy-Nagy, *Vorankündigung der Bauhausbücher vierseitiges Faltblatt*, 1924.

structures by Donald Judd, and other minimal art promoters, all demonstrate the same desire for minimization as is apparent in Malevich's *Black Square on a White Background*, in Loos' rejection of decoration, in Marcel Breuer's tubular systems, or in Max Bill's *gute Form* of rationalism, among other celebrated examples. All of these works display a predominantly anti-illusionist attitude, aimed at expressing the essential by avoiding any decorative elements and using primary and repetitive structures. The purpose is to eliminate all allusions, to liberate art from any referential, representative, or metaphorical function, which is why the shapes used can be instantly perceived in their entirety. This kind of art speaks to the intellect.

Simplicity as a process of expressing the essential, removing decoration, and imitating the reproducibility of technology and the expressive rigor of utensils was clearly a stylistic goal of the 20th century. The expression *gute Form* of German functionalism, applied to the field of functional design, has survived through periods of high complexity and iconic intensity by mutating its genes. The rationalist simplicity of architecture and design has been interpreted in different ways and for different uses.

However, simplicity is an extremely complicated and unnatural problem. The simplicity of minimalism conflicts with semantic aphasia and with superstition about simple things. Eloquent simplicity takes great effort to achieve, but can never be a starting point: "Art and architecture are not simple, they can only become simple,"[20] states Vittorio Gregotti in an interpretative essay on architecture from within. Exploration of the

[20] Vittorio Gregotti, *Desde el interior de la arquitectura. Un ensayo de interpretación* [Architecture from within. An Interpretative Essay]. Ediciones Peninsula, Barcelona, 1983, page 94.

simplicity evident in minimalist art, architecture, and music requires an understanding of the contradiction it presents, and must therefore open a debate on its limitations that can tackle the profound difficulties of our time.

Freed of the superfluous, minimalist sculpture, architecture, or choreography is not simple because of the elementary geometry of its shapes, or because the logical connections between its parts are evident. It is simple because its parts communicate as necessary, reciprocally with one another, and respecting the sense of the specific architectural or scenic solution. This spatial condition of minimalist aesthetics does have its precedents and forerunners, but above all it is an essential part of our contemporary aesthetic vocabulary and of the sensitive relations between art and architecture that shape our environment.[21]

Max Bill, *Wall Clock*.

[21] Josep M. Montaner, *La modernidad superada* [Modernity Overtaken]. Gustavo Gil, Barcelona, 1997.

The Minimalist Condition

The minimalist inheritance, and that of pop art, are powerful symbols of the aesthetic crisis that pervaded the mid-20th century. Rather than a style, minimalism is a conceptual and technical tool used to create a space constructed by the alternatives it condemns.

The minimal look, with the bluntness of its elementary shapes, which became established among American artists at the end of the 1960s, is characteristic of those who place their work between painting and sculpture, between abstraction and figuration, between architecture and sculpture, and essentially between any other dogmatic category. It is a radical and systematic search, a kind of art that is both idealistic and materialistic and defines a new condition for modernity: post-modern art in all its multiple forms. Geometric paintings, Peter Halley's so-called neo-geo, for example, are concerned with lines and pure volumes in the same way as minimalism, but move in a different direction, expressing an interest in the cultural meanings of these same structures.

Peter Halley, *White Cell with Conduit*, 1987, acrylic day-glo and roll-a-tex on canvas.

Hal Foster, like Rosalind Krauss, has written most prolifically about the influence of minimal and pop art on art in the 1980s and 1990s, and points to examples among international artists like Hans Haacke, Barbara Kruger, Allan McCollum, Jeff Koons, Haim Steinbach, or Félix González-Torres. He writes: "One way of demonstrating the role played by minimalism is to see it and pop art as two kinds of responses to the same situation in the dialectics of modernism and mass culture."[22]

Minimalism begins, with Judd, as an interpretation of late modernity, as a new frontier and a new freedom in art, opening the way to post-modernist thinking. As an analysis of perception, minimalism is also an analysis of the conditions of perception. This analysis gradually leads to criticism of art spaces (museums, galleries), of conventional art exhibitions, of its condition as a commodity, and of the strategies of representation and their influence on the constitution of contemporary subjects. Minimalism had had an impact on the entire art scene by the end of the 20th century, and crossed its own conceptual boundaries. Minimalism is not a break with modernist practice but a split. Minimalist art concentrates on creating new objects that are beyond any function and comply only with their own principles of internal organization. Minimalist objects are, therefore, defined by their artistic context or space, which also determines the viewer's approach and attitude toward the work of art.

[22] Hal Foster, "The essence of minimalism," text included in Gregory Battcock's publication *Minimal Art: A Critical Anthology*. E.P. Dutton, New York, 1968; University of California Press, 1995.

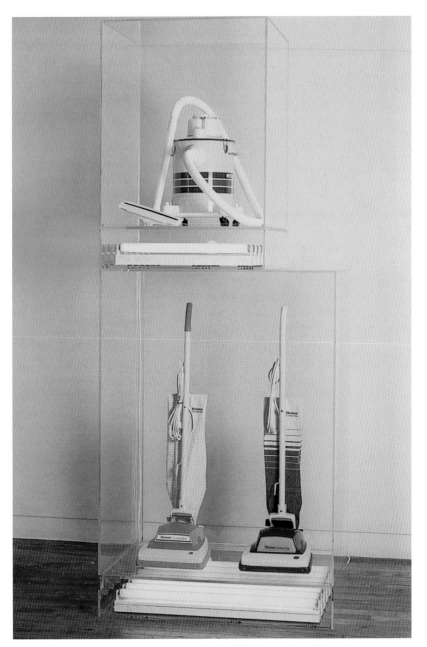

Jeff Koons, *New Hoover Convertibles. New Shelton Wet/Dry displaced double decker*, 1981–1987, Plexiglas, vacuum cleaners and fluorescent tubes.

Lawrence Weiner, *A 36" x 36" Removal to the Lathing or Support Wall of Plaster or Wallboard from a Wall*, 1969/1983, The Siegelaub Collection & Archives.

The minimalist period was marked by a legendary exhibition called "When attitudes become form" (1969), organized at Bern Art Gallery by the critic Harald Szeeman. Szeeman defined post-minimalism in art as the convergence of the formal language of minimalism with the strategies of conceptual art. At that exhibition, Lawrence Weiner produced *A 36" x 36" Removal to the Lathing or Support Wall of Plaster or Wallboard from a Wall*, which showed the inside of a wall from which a 36-inch square of plaster had been removed. By doing so, the artist radicalized and institutionalized – in terms of the museum or art exhibition space – the minimalist debate about the condition of pictures on walls. The function of artistic spaces is questioned, because these same spaces could be considered minimalist sculptures on a wider scale when artists use them as active structures. This is what Daniel Buren did when he started to restrict his work to three fundamental factors: the specific place, a concrete situation, and a limited duration.

The French art of **Daniel Buren**, like the essence of American minimalism, is there to ask questions, not to provide answers.

Daniel Buren, *Site in Situ N° 1*, 1984, wood, tarpaulin and paint. Neues Museum Wesenburg Bremen. Dr. Klaus Lafrenz Collection.

At first sight, his method is minimalist: he makes rigorous use of two-color stripes and pays more attention to structure than content. However, rather than pursuing formal self-referential issues, he is more interested in establishing a cool, calm, and collected dialog between the work of art and the viewer, which may trigger new questions about the artistic space of the museum and about art spaces in general. As Buren himself explains: "My work aims to create a public, I am not addressing an existing one."

Although we may spot essential differences in content, and in the use of minimalist language, the minimalist influence on international art in the 1980s and 1990s is undeniable. For example, Michelangelo Pistoletto's reversible structures, Robert Ryman's white surfaces, Susana Solano's sculptural fences, Philippe Cazal's serial boxes with inscriptions, On Kawara's date paintings, Fred Sandback's sculptural lines, and James Turrell's spaces of luminous perception demonstrate the many different paths taken by minimalist artists.[23]

Even the works of **Félix González-Torres**, which are more strictly minimalist, are influenced by the historical weight of

[23] The minimalist inheritance is analyzed in the catalog for the "Minimal-Maximal" exhibition held at the Galician Contemporary Art Center, Santiago de Compostela, 1999.

Michelangelo Pistoletto, *Struttura per parlare in piedi*, 1965–1966, iron, varnish.

James Turrell, *Skyspace I*, 1972, interior light with open sky. Panza Collection.

James Turrell, *Skeet*, 1990.

minimal art, confronting the viewer with a procedure that is radical in its simplicity and apparent "lack of art." His work *Untitled (Republican years)* (1992) consists of a stack of white paper with a double black margin. The geometric shape and anonymous nature of the work, as well as the precision with which the stack is formed and its industrial association, are reminiscent of minimalism, but González-Torres adds to his work new experiences for the viewer. In this case the paper can be taken away by the public – like the piles of sweets in other works – and therefore the artwork itself becomes less un-changeable and self-sufficient than Judd's boxes or Andre's floors. The work retains its self-referential quality, but can be transformed by the viewer and is legitimated as a sculpture by the paradox of its dual formal entity: museum sculpture on the one hand, and souvenir for the viewer to take home on the other. In his work, González-Torres creates a new presence and condition for minimalist sculpture, as Judd and Morris formu-lated it. In his case, the presence relies on the willingness and action of the viewer, who gradually deconstructs the work until it disappears. Equally, the concept of place varies according to the location of the object and its ephemeral nature; even the stomachs of the viewers eating their sweets become places.

Félix González-Torres, *Untitled (Republican years)*, 1992, offset print on paper, limited edition. Sprengel Museum Collection, Hanover.

While González-Torres uses minimal art in a new way to deal with more personal concepts – love, sexuality, sickness – the work of German artist **Hans Haacke** uses it in a more political way. His art is one of compromise, expressing itself on specific political matters in a minimalist guise. Pieces like *Kondensationsboden* (1970), a see-through Plexiglas cube, are expansions of minimalist practice. The hermetically sealed box contains water. Any small variations in temperature and pressure in the room cause the water to heat up and cool down slowly, condensing as steam on the glass surface and forming droplets, which eventually fall back into the mass of water and disappear. This cycle takes place continuously, making the viewer aware of a process occurring in real time. This means having to concentrate, having to approach the work in a different way: to see, think, and imagine in real time in order to consider specific transformations that are not immediately visible, would escape cursory observation, and go beyond the strict minimal art concept of just "being there." It is a question of accepting a kind of art that performs processes that exist independently of the viewer, but are part of a complex reciprocal relationship.

Hans Haacke, *Kondensationsboden*, 1970, Plexiglas, water. Neues Museum Wesenburg Bremen. Carl Gastner Collection.

Another eloquent example of the conceptual diversity of minimalism in the 1980s and 1990s is the work of **Haim Steinbach**, which displays the way in which pop art and minimal art have creatively merged as a result of the aesthetic evolution of recent years. In the 1980s, his work was characterized by sets of objects that allude to both "high" and "low" culture, which use and reformulate minimalism to detect a new artistic condition.

Haim Steinbach, *Supremely Black*, mixed process construction.

Steinbach's first reductionist paintings consisted of geometric signs grouped together inside the square perimeter of the canvas. By doing this he questioned the notion of the surface and of the place in which the sense of the artistic object should be understood. He uses the place to decontextualize it, and builds window boxes, shelves, or containers in which to arrange unrelated objects to create certain combinations of color or shape, or other pictorial values used in a random way. Perhaps his most minimalist trait is the way in which he systematically erodes the concept of work. The construction of his pieces requires the minimum amount of physical effort, and his workshop is an office connected to a warehouse where he stores the materials he finds or buys for his work. This behavior relates him to a whole generation of pop artists and minimalists and to their revision of the concepts of taste, perception, tradition, and market. Steinbach's work clearly shows the pure state of the object in a referential vacuum. His art defies interpretation because the objects reveal the subliminal spaces in the metaphor. The object displays the great question mark of modern culture and survival in the echo of the questions it poses.

The influence of minimalism can also be seen in architecture and design, where it has brought about a review and an expansion of theory and practice. An important starting point for the revision that took place in the 1960s was the architecture of **Louis Kahn**, with its idiosyncratic take on the modernist legacy, in which he uses his own unmistakable language of strictly geometrical and structural discipline in all details and volumes. This can be seen at the Yale Art Gallery (1952–1954). It is also apparent in the work of **I.M. Pei**, as in the distinctive intersected volumes of the National Art Gallery in Washington (1971–1978), with their principle of formal economy and identical geometric

I.M. Pei, Louvre Pyramid, Paris, 1989.

Louis Kahn, *Kimbell Museum*, Fort Worth, Texas, 1967–1972 © Klaus-Peter Gast.

pathos. Geometric rigor, technical precision, powerful materiality, unity and simplicity, scale distortion, prevalence of the structural form, and avoidance of any historical reference generate a powerful minimalist phenomenology which affects and stimulates a multitude of interpretations in the currents of art and architecture of our time.[24]

The concept of "less is more" makes it possible to achieve a greater monumentality. If Kahn's work recalls that of Mies van der Rohe in order to attack it, the Japanese architect **Tadao Ando** also refers to it when he approaches it in a way more closely connected to the concept of place. His concrete buildings are both open and closed, finding their unity in the intense use of a very limited number of shapes and materials, attempting to achieve the maximum with the minimum. The Water Chapel in Hokkaido (1989) is an example of how minimalist architecture and Japanese haiku can awaken our senses in the serenity of space in which man, God, and nature coexist.

The beauty of emptiness, of the pure present at its most minimalist, achieves an extraordinary power in the architectural spaces of **Luis Barragán**. The abstract composition of walls, colors, and shadows at his own home in Mexico DF (1947) are the basis for an individual reductionist language, a poetry of silence and architectural isolation with the mute bluntness of elementary geometry. This sculptural approach is also apparent in the volumes and in the precision of materials used by **Souto de Moura** in the cultural center of the secretariat for the State of Oporto (1981–1989). In all of Souto de Moura's work there are implicit minimalist references to the sculptures of Donald Judd and the architecture of Mies van der Rohe and Luis Barragán.

---

[24] The artistic reduction in architecture is analyzed by Ignasi de Solá-Morales in *Diferencias. Topografía de la arquitectura contemporánea* [Differences. The Topography of Contemporary Architecture]. Gustavo Gili, Barcelona, 1995.

Tadao Ando, water chapel, Hokkaido, Japan, 1989.

Luis Barragán, Tacubaya, Mexico, 1947.

The buildings by the Brazilian **Paulo Mendes da Rocha**, with their vast, reinforced-concrete structural and geometric features, bear traces of minimalism in their attention to the concept of place and presence. The São Paulo Museum of Sculpture (1983–1994) is an open structure consisting of a giant concrete girder, a purely minimalist sculpture. **Lina Bo Bardi** also moves beyond the limits of modern art while respecting its basic principles, creating architecture in Brazil that displays strict rationalism, simplification, and repetition in an exuberant way. Her designs do not propose a new kind of formalism, a new form of architecture, but a method for overcoming the limitations of modernity using the richness of the present. Hers is an abstract, vernacular kind of modernity, which plays with Miesian models and with the colors and smells of vegetation or the sounds of the surrounding area, integrating functionalism with the richness and creativity of popular art. The São Paulo Museum of Art, with its fantastic public space in the foyer, is one of the most emblematic works of Bo Bardi's vitalist minimalism.

Lina Bo Bardi, foyer of the Museum of Art, São Paulo, Brazil, 1960–1969.

The architecture of **Jean Nouvel**, like that of his compatriot **Dominique Perrault** (French Library, Paris, 1994), also recreates – in the cold and static transparency of materials – shapes that allude to the constructivism of the avant-garde as much as to the modular forms of Sol LeWitt or the intangible spaces of Dan Flavin.

Dominique Perrault, French National Library, Paris, 1996. © Photo by Georges Fessy.

The prevalence of structural shapes, understood as aesthetic and constructive elements, reaches new levels of monumentality in the works of architects like **Aldo Rossi** and **Giorgio Grassi**. Rossi's architecture is based on clarity, because clarity is an attribute of reason. The repetition of rigorously geometric elements – low columns, windows – creates a poetry that reveals the influence of Swiss tradition and purism, and the erosion of minimalism.

Francisco Javier Sáenz de Oíza, Atlantic Center of Modern Art, 1989. Las Palmas, Canary Islands.

This search for unity, achieved by the use of few shapes and materials, which goes beyond minimalism, is also apparent in the sculptural nature of works by the architects **Jordi Garcés** and **Enric Sòria** (water storage tanks in Santa María de Barberá, Spain, 1971), **Herzog/De Meuron** (Goetz Art Gallery in Munich, Germany, 1989–1992) or **Abalos/Herreros** (Simancas Sports Center, Valladolid, Spain, 1991). Without the ostentatious use of high technology or of any decoration, the designs produced by these teams of architects characterize the spread of a new minimalist tradition across the world.

Garcés-Sòria, Santa Mara de Barberá, Spain, 1971.

There is one kind of minimalism that expresses itself on a large scale, in the sculptural value of huge but simple shapes, like skyscrapers. Another kind of minimalism can be perceived in the nakedness and simplicity of interiors, in the quality of technical detail and in the domestic perception of materiality. Essentially, minimalism manifests itself as much in a condensed style of expression as in the simplification of shapes, as much in the search for transparency and immateriality as in the creation of solid, blunt, stable, and gestaltic objects.

Jean Nouvel, *Arca, BAO*, aluminum.

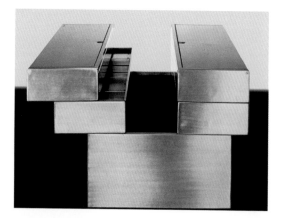

Scott Burton, *Soft geometric chair,* foam, cloth.

Contemporary design has also borrowed from the minimalism of illustrious avant-garde predecessors – furniture by Rietveld and Breuer – to reconvert the language of geometry. The rigorous linearity of Marco Zanuso's Quaderno table (1970) for Zanotta, the Misura de Superstudio furniture collection, the impeccable designs of Vico Magistretti, the formal coolness of the Less table by Jean Nouvel, or the work of Massimo Vignelli, who specializes in dramatic variations of scale and size, bring new meaning to the minimalist condition in our culture.

Furniture by Scott Burton, particularly his foam-rubber pieces for the Swiss company Vitra International, can also be considered to be minimalist sculpture on account of its strict geometric construction. Further examples of minimalism might include the transparent structures of designs by Shiro Kuramata, such as his How High the Moon armchair.

Shiro Kuramata, How High the Moon chair, metal and steel tubes.

Minimalism is also apparent in the field of music, dance, and stage design. Two key composers in the history of musical minimalism are Erik Satie and Darius Milhaud. The extravagance of their work, and their repetition of certain bars, set a pattern for minimal music in the 1960s and for the exploration of its style of expression.

Electroacoustic music and personalities like John Cage create a new relationship between the creator and his audience. Human and mechanical intermediaries disappear; there is no performer, no score, no traditional script. At Woodstock, in 1952, accompanied by the pianist David Tudor, Cage first performed the work entitled "4' 33", a silent piece in three movements: the performer comes onstage, opens the lid of the piano and waits, timing the duration of each movement. Four minutes and 30 seconds of silence later, he says goodbye to the audience and leaves the stage. With this experiment, Cage's intention was not to show a particular path but to value the knowledge there is in other paths.

Empty sound spaces, silence, or repetition were used in new musical structures, which were defined as minimalist from 1976 onward, in the works of Michael Nyman and Philip Glass. Their music is simply based on the continuous repetition of a tune or of short figures, normally diatonic, in the interaction of which slow and gradual rhythmic and harmonic transformations are introduced. Minimalist music is not the kind of music you listen to but one that you enter and leave. Musicians who came after Cage, and were influenced by Zen philosophy and Oriental music, generated other reductionist coordinates for their art. While La Monte Young takes Japanese theater and Indian ragas as inspiration, Terry Riley refers to avant-garde music and jazz, Philip Glass works assiduously with Indian music, and Steve Reich adopts the rhythms of African music.

The conventional idea of musical composition as a pre-established whole no longer exists, and repetitive composition is essentially a process whose function is not to represent anything other than itself. The music opts for generating a present at every moment. For minimalists in the 1960s and 1970s, the involvement of the audience was fundamental because the listener was to perceive and take an active part in the construction.

Musical action in unusual spaces, far from conventional scenarios, improvisation and its investigation of time, space, and the environment, are the basic elements of minimalist music and its relationship with dance, stage design, or art.[25] Philip Glass worked with Robert Wilson in 1976 on the creation of a monumental theatrical piece called *Einstein on the Beach*. La Monte Young frequently works with Terry Riley and the choreographer Ann Halprin. John Cage's relationship with dancer Merce Cunningham also represents the collaboration between different forms of artistic interpretation that was so highly valued by the minimalists.

[25] Read the article by Manona Sagarra Trias and Joaquín Turina Gómez, "Del menys el millor" [The Best from the Least] in *Less is More*. Catalan College of Architects, Barcelona, 1996.

Cesc Gelabert.

In contemporary dance, pieces by Merce Cunningham, Yvonne Rainer, Anne Teresa de Keersmaeker, Trista Brown, or Lucilda Childs reduce movement to its minimum expression. Their repetitive sequences draw the spectator into a dynamic experience similar to that of viewers admiring a minimalist sculpture, walking around it and looking at it from different positions.

Minimalist references can also be found in literature, photography, cinema, and fashion. In fact, there is no new artistic movement that has not been understood and classified from the standpoint of minimalism. The issues first raised by minimal art and the minimalist condition can continue to lay new and useful paths for the future. The questions that minimalism used to ask continue to be asked today.

Bernd and Hilla Becher, *Typology Watertowers*, 1972, black and white photographs.

Applied Minimalism

Fashion
Design
Architecture
Interiors

Applied Minimalism: Introduction

This second chapter contains an anthology of work in the fields of fashion, object design, furniture, interior design, and architecture. All these areas have been influenced by this new trend, which has lasted for more than 40 years.

Minimalism is not a technique for cutting the cost of a creation or for speeding up the construction process. On the contrary, projects influenced by it are often complicated to build, highly detailed, and made with expensive materials. They create an aura of serenity and great sophistication. The absence of redundant elements generally means that great care has been taken with the components actually included in them. To complement architectural works like the ones illustrated, interior designers and decorators often prefer modern furniture, which may have hard or soft lines, be made of fine or synthetic materials, and in pale or vivid colors. It is the absence of decoration that is the essential feature of any minimalist work.

Minimalism can be found in the work of John Pawson and Claudio Silvestrin in England, Hiroyuki Arima in Japan, Peter Marino in New York, Artec in rural France, and Eduardo Castillo in the remote southern areas of Chile. How is it that this way of doing things, this sensitivity for materials and spaces, light and textures, can be found in places so far apart, in environments as diverse as a boutique in Madison Avenue and a country church in a faraway field?

The result of a minimalist work does not necessarily depend on the use of elaborate production methods, advanced technology or specific materials, but on a purely rational process which can even be distinguished from its construction. Perhaps this is why this way of doing things, this design sensitivity, is so easy to import, particularly considering that it has evolved at a time when the effects of globalization (in the economy) are being felt in the fields of culture and mass consumption.

There are some specific sculptural and aesthetic features which recur in the field of minimalism: abstraction, order, neutrality, elementary shapes, anti-illusionism, minimum formal complexity, and the importance attributed to material, used structurally or as a covering.

Lighting is one of the most important aspects of minimalism, both in architecture and interior design. Overhead or indirect lighting, diffuse lighting, and points of light can expand a space, wash over a wall, highlight certain elements, light up a path, show the passage of time, and reflect colors. It is interesting to see how the use of light filters, very light white fabrics, translucent glass, or different kinds of screens to diffuse light, make objects look as if they can defy the laws of gravity. Spaces become dreamy (as in Moerkerke House by John Pawson) and shadowless. Translucent materials have the ability to suggest contours rather than to show them. The light they allow through blurs the edges of objects, making them look as if they might dissolve into space. Timber laminate panels have a similar effect. Appearing solid from a distance, they can be perforated in all kinds of different ways without altering the final look of the surface, which is harmonized by this filtering of the light (as in Sirch Timber Warehouse by Baumschlager & Eberle).

Fashion

Minimalism and Fashion

More an Attitude than a Fashion

The level now attained by aesthetic minimalism in the field of fashion is not the result of a new trend but of a series of artistic, aesthetic, and social circumstances, which have combined to perpetuate a style or form of creation inspired by minimalism. Often called purism in the business, it is one of the most lasting trends in the world of contemporary fashion.

The appearance of minimal art in the 1960s formed the principles of this new way of doing things, which had artistic abstraction and lack of decoration as its conceptual sources, and classic Japanese austerity as well as modern North American functionalism as its direct aesthetic references.

In aesthetic terms, minimalism appears to be a logical reaction to the excesses of fashion: hippy (1960s), glam (1970s), and punk (1980s). It proposes a break with these trends, suggesting a series of strategies inherited from the modernist movement and minimal art. These include the absence of ornamentation, the use of new technologies in the production of materials and fabrics, the exaltation of fabric as a raw material, and the emblematic use of a very limited range of colors, straight lines, and objects. These circumstances, combined with the growing trend to place the responsibility for beauty not only on clothing but also on physical exercise and advanced cosmetics, inspired fashion designers to develop simple, anonymous, and sophisticated garments at the end of the 20th century, when the world seemed to need a rest.

© Photo Peter Knapp   Sipa Press

A Return to Classicism

Many people define the presence of minimalist aesthetic in fashion as a return to classicism, a place of safety from which to deal effectively with the excesses of the 1970s and 1980s. Classic Greco-Roman expression uses a language of proportions, pure geometry, and schematic simplicity. By applying these principles and making use of new materials and technologies, pioneering designers of minimalist art, like Zoran, created apparently austere, classical, and uncomplicated styles, achieving great success in the world of high fashion during the 1970s and 1980s.

Goe More

Homage to Modernity

The rational and technical revision of classicism proposed by modernity exploited the opportunities offered by the break with history. The leitmotif was "maximum reduction in elements for maximum aesthetic effect." The modern artistic avant-garde designed clothing inspired by military uniforms, work clothing and sportswear. Coco Chanel was the first fashion designer to incorporate sportswear ideas into high fashion by producing simple and elegant lines.

Howard Shickler/FineArt

Lipnitzki-Viollet

Japanese Austerity

The Contemporary Tradition

In the field of fashion, the basic principles of Japanese culture have remained intact, despite the external changes experienced as a result of the contact it has had with the West since the end of the 19th century. The Japanese have traditionally associated pure lines and honest simplicity with the concept of beauty. Purity is an essential component of Shintoism, and simplicity is one of the ideals of Zen doctrine. Economy of the means of expression extends to Japanese artistic and cultural traditions which are alive today, such as haiku, bonsai, origami, and the tea ceremony, the aim of which is to remove everything but the elements strictly required to display the essential beauty of the object or form.

© Albert Watson

The Kimono

The harmonious coexistence of the traditional and modern is probably the most notable feature of modern Japanese society. The kimono, which simply means dress in Japanese, is the garment most symbolic of Japan, and the most palpable proof that Japanese clothing has not been unaffected by the trend of eliminating the superfluous. This traditional garment is produced from a *tan*, a piece of cloth of a set length and identical width, which is successively folded to fit the body. This unisex garment is used day and night for various occasions and activities, fulfilling many of the principles pursued by the minimalist movement at the end of the 20th century. However, the fact that it bears no relation to the environment and lifestyle of contemporary Japan has led designers like Issey Miyake to reformulate its shape but not its principles, which have even been exported to the West.

© Noriaki Yokosuka,
courtesy of Issey Miyake

Japan Conquers the West

The Japanese influence on art and other creative disciplines is not new. During the second half of the 19th century, postcards of Japanese etchings fascinated artists like Degas and Van Gogh, and revolutionized painting. The history of modern Japanese art could be seen as the result of comings and goings between the modern West and traditional Japan. The arrival in Paris of Kenzo and Issey Miyake in the1960s, and the presence of designers like Kansai Yamamoto, Junko Koshino, and Junko Shimada in the 1970s, confirmed the French fascination with

Japanese culture. It was the work of Yohji Yamamoto and Rei Kawakubo (Comme des Garçons), however, that marked the beginning of a serious reflection on the traditional fashion of wide shoulders and high heels that had dominated the West for decades. By creating a series of designs displaying reserve and modesty, creating a truly modern look of unembellished wrap-around garments, flat shoes and no makeup, these designers initially astonished the critics, but soon won them over.

Poupées Russes collection, 1989.
© Yohji Yamamoto

Issey Miyake

From the outset, Miyake opted for simple, functional, and economical designs, contravening the principles of traditional high-fashion tailoring. His capacity for synthesis and abstraction was inspired by both traditional and modern Japanese aesthetics. Miyake's designs rely greatly on fabric quality. This has led him to develop new materials (from bamboo to metals) using craft techniques in textiles, which, thanks to his efforts, have become industrial processes. Miyake sees his creations as objects with a purity that makes them both avant-gardist and timeless. Of all Japanese avant-garde artists, he is the one who has really understood the total concept of fashion, and converted his designs into artistic as well as commercial successes. Miyake has exhibited his collections in various museums and art galleries around the world.

© The Victoria and Albert Museu

Miyake Design Studio

Yohji Yamamoto

Yamamoto's first collections in the early 1980s were greeted with astonishment and excitement by the world of fashion. His proposal of an androgynous look, at a time when the prevalent female image was that of the *femme fatale*, heralded a radical revision of the concept of fashion in the West. This provocative proposition, made in the spirit of honest Japanese simplicity, was to characterize all his creations, and developed his identity in the world of fashion to the point that some refer to him as a living legend. Yamamoto's creations are based on the themes of movement and functionality, to which the designer applies his boundless imagination and perfect tailoring. The purist and controlled vision of this Japanese designer, who has now settled in Paris, is not limited to fashion but extends to life itself. This view reflects on his staff and on his points of sale, which are veritable temples to Japanese minimalism.

© Nick Knight, for Yohji Yamamoto

Rei Kawakubo (Comme des Garçons)

Kawakubo's work is closely linked to that of Yohji Yamamoto. Both were responsible for importing the new image of an avant-gardist Japan into Western fashion at the end of the 1970s. Kawakubo's severe dresses, lacking in any kind of ornamentation and distinguished by the geometry of their lines and the beauty of their monochrome fabrics, defined the new, apparently nonchalant, look of her creations. Kawakubo is a fabric sculptor who produces conceptual and austere garments and who, like Yamamoto, never neglects any detail of her designs, boutiques, shows, or publications.

J. Casano/Stills/Studio X

North American Functionalism

Equality and Uniformity

American style was born in the newly independent USA, where people needed to clothe themselves with simple, handmade garments suitable for work. Self-sufficiency was a value promoted by George Washington and of markedly austere and rural communities like the Amish and Quakers. Ostentation was disapproved of in a nation dedicated to emphasizing its newly gained democracy, and in which simplicity was elevated to a virtue. Equality and uniformity of work and army clothing, all made of denim, were the principal cultural influences of the American style, whose greatest legacies in casual wear have been jeans and khakis.

Nick Knight

Nick Knight

The City as a Backdrop

Simple aesthetics, inspired by open-air activities, are the origin of a casual, spontaneous, and anonymous kind of fashion, which soon conquered the cities and became the "city look." During the 1980s, American designers developed this concept to extremes, using it everywhere to create essential day/night or work/leisure garments with simple, clean lines, for a more functional and less formal look than traditional, more structured clothing. Cities like New York were the Meccas of the city look. Offices allowed "dress-down Fridays" every week, and the streets were transformed into showcases of minimalist fashion.

Pepe Botella

Zoran

Many people would not hesitate to name Ladicorbic Zoran as the first designer who purposely and deliberately introduced minimalist sensitivity in his designs. Originally from Yugoslavia and trained in architecture, he aimed to remove all accessories and details that might taint the sobriety of his garments. Zoran developed a wardrobe of basic, comfortably structured clothing in neutral colors. The apparent simplicity of his designs actually required a complex kind of construction and extremely good-quality fabrics.

Albert Watson.
© Condé Nast Publications Ltd.

Calvin Klein

Klein, who became famous in the mid-1970s, created many of the most convincing fashion concepts of the late 20th century. His success is down to the sophistication of his clothing and also to the devastating efficiency of his marketing strategy. His global concept of a simple, functional, and provocative kind of fashion has earned him the unquestionable respect of young, medium- to high-spending consumers in cities across the world. Klein has created an empire that is quite unprecedented in this sector, selling ready-to-wear clothing, watches, perfumes, and underwear from Hong Kong to Prague. Inheriting the American tradition in the design of work clothing and uniforms, Klein started his first collections with jeans and khakis. His skill lies in an ability to add a touch of class to traditional American functionalism, developing a sporty look of simple lines that fulfills contemporary requirements, using durable, high-resistance fabrics. Klein is the inventor of "street style" and, apart from transforming his designs into an extraordinarily successful business, he has brought American style into the circle of international fashion.

Angeli/Pandis/Telepress

Donna Karan

The simple values that characterized American style during the 1970s and 1980s were soon applied to women's fashions. Styles were created for women who were taking on increasing responsibilities in the world of work. The designs helped active, powerful, urban women feel as comfortable at a breakfast meeting as at a cocktail party, by providing them with a classic wardrobe of "essentials," which Karan proposed for every season. Consisting of eight indispensable garments that could be combined with one another, the ranges allowed women to carry everything they needed to deal with any situation in one suitcase. Karan's casual style and subdued colors simply confirmed that Americans are the best at designing essential clothing and producing financially viable collections. The DKNY ready-to-wear line diversified into jeans, menswear, and children's clothes, in addition to accessories and perfumes.

Miyake Design Studio

Peter Lindberg. © Donna Karan

Marc Jacobs

Collaboration between young designers and traditional fashion houses has been essential for commercial survival, as well as necessary for innovation. The presence of Marc Jacobs as the creative director of Louis Vuitton has allowed the development of ready-to-wear collections that are beautifully simple and full of modern references, introducing pop images into one of the most traditional bastions of fashion.

Michael Kors

Like Jacobs at Louis Vuitton, Kors has collaborated with Céline. His fun, sexy, and practical style of neutral and vivid colors can be defined as poor in form but rich in texture. Simple and well-cut products made of cashmere, leather, or silk have captivated high-spending customers, who find casual but elegant sophistication in his minimalist chic.

The European Alternative

After the Excesses

At the end of almost three decades of extravagant fashions inspired by flower power, glam rock and punk music, many designers turned to designing clothes dictated more by function and materials than fashion. In a context of technological progress and of a global society turning its back on the excesses of the 1980s, minimalism found fertile ground in fashion to consolidate its uncompromising style. Clothes, furniture, and buildings were reduced to their essential forms, developing a somewhat cold and sophisticated look, characterized by functionality. The use of single colors was another reaction against the profusion of color in previous fashions. Black, white, and a range of neutral colors became the preferred palette of this aesthetic purity, which reserved other hues for the occasional controlled touch of color or for sportswear (another version of the minimalist reaction).

Giorgio Armani

Giorgio Armani has proudly inherited the beautiful sobriety of Italian style, evident in the most perfectly designed products of the 20th century, from typewriters to cars. After working with Nino Cerruti, Armani revolutionized the world of fashion in the mid-1970s, revising the traditional concept of men's suits by introducing new fabrics and combining neutral colors. Later on, he incorporated these changes into his women's wear, offering greater freedom to modern, liberal, and active women. From the outset, his collections could be defined as urban, dynamic, and androgynous. The perfect cut and exquisite finish of his garments, produced under strict control, ensure the unbeatable luxury of his collections, which are always sophisticated but never ostentatious. Emporio Armani, set up in 1981, now markets unmistakably cool and elegant style.

Max Mara

Characterized by the incomparable features of Italian style – classic lines, excellent quality, and impeccable detail – Max Mara's collections have always demonstrated the virtues of simplicity and elegance.

Steve Mersel, courtesy of Max Mara

Jil Sander

This German designer detected a need for modesty in fashion and made it her benchmark. Her work is characterized by a harsh and contemporary purity, which is greatly inspired by the severity and rigor of men's suits. Jil Sander has followed in the footsteps of Armani, Klein, and Karan in terms of their search for sophistication, but has taken a step beyond by using the latest fabrics to give her designs a strictly modern look.

Antonio Miró

The best way to describe this designer's work is to use his own words: "I like simple and useful objects, produced using authentic materials, which will accompany me in my daily life and grow old with me... like the clothes I design, which are comfortable and austere, and fit so well that you could easily forget you were wearing them."

Xavier Ribera

Futurism and Minimalist Deconstruction
The New Standard

Fashion design in the 1990s was mostly aimed at satisfying the daily requirements of work and leisure in a way that was functional and austere. In the light of this new standard, young designers ventured into futurism and used alternative methods of construction. Despite the intensity of experimentation and their great imagination, the prevalent style has continued to be neoclassical, based on pure geometry and schematic simplicity. Black and white, combined with neutral tones, continue to be the colors most favored by these designers, who never hesitate to use new materials while remaining within the boundaries of haute couture and *prêt-à-porter*.

Peter Lindberg. © Donna Karan

Martin Margiela

Martin Margiela's avant-gardist, theoretical, and experimental work, carried out in a spirit of deconstruction and reinvention, earned him a place in fashion at the end of the 20th century for his honestly brutal (or brutally honest?) style. The skills of this passionate designer led him to collaborate with Hermès, one of the temples of classical fashion, an event that was greeted with great excitement and enthusiasm.

Martine Sitbon

Inspired by the London scene in the 1960s, Sitbon has developed a unisex, uninhibited, and sophisticated look for women, and has also feminized her menswear collections. Light and androgynous silhouettes are her hallmark. The quality of her work has led her to contribute to Chloé's ready-to-wear collections.

Miyake Design Studio

Helmut Lang

This Austrian designer has one of the severest images in the world of fashion. He displays the disillusionment of the younger generation by applying an unprecedented rigor to his designs and using an extremely limited range of colors. The use of synthetic fabrics is another aspect of his work, which allows him to modernize by ensuring the rigid construction of his designs. Lang believes that perfect clothes should never irritate you. He also believes that rigor and imagination are not incompatible, and bases his work on these principles.

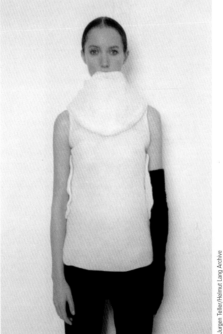

Jurgen Teller/Helmut Lang Archive

Jurgen Teller/Helmut Lang Archive

Ann Demeulemeester

Some of the most representative images of fashion at the end of the 20th century can be found in the work of this talented and confident designer, whose garments are intended to satisfy her customers rather than please the critics. Her characteristically androgynous and mystifying designs, her deliberate carelessness, her eagerness to display contrasts, and her taste for the color black define one of the most original designers of the 1990s.

Dirk Bikkembergs

The work of this Belgian designer displays the potential for experimentation that exists in menswear. Dark colors, heavy fabrics, and solid silhouettes characterize his menswear collections, which propose designs that go far beyond the stale suit-and-tie formula. His look is full of allusions to military and workmen's clothing, demonstrating his search for new variations within the boundaries of traditional elegance.

Michael Compte, courtesy of Dirk Bikkembergs

Eric Berger

His admiration for simple and stylish American sportswear and the androgynous coolness of London in the 1960s combine to produce garments that reduce details, accessories, and redundant elements to a minimum.

Mario Testino for Visionaire "Chic," Sept. 1997

Costume National

Ennio Capasa designs clothes for this range that are a synthesis of haute couture and street wear, and bases his work on the quality of materials. As a result of his collaboration with Yohji Yamamoto, his work is marked by severity but softened by the traditional sensuality and elegance of Italian design.

Nathaniel Goldberg, Paris

Hussein Chalayan

Chalayan is interested in clothes rather than fashion. The sinister and mysterious look of his collections has earned him a reputation for darkness, which he has never hesitated to exploit.

Marcus Tomlinson. © Hussein Chalayan

Accessories

Footwear

Traditional designers like Prada continue to dominate the world of footwear, while experimenting with new technical processes and producing discreetly elegant and sumptuous collections. Under Muccia's direction, Prada even displays signs of minimalism, with designs reflecting the changing times. The greatest advances have been made in the field of sports fashions, where comfort, weight reduction, and greater resistance of materials are the main objectives which designers aim to achieve. The trend toward reducing accessories to gain greater functionality has led to the development of slip-on shoes with no laces, sometimes only partially covered, to free the foot from having to make unnecessary effort.

The leather goods sector maintains close links with the directors of the various fashion houses and their collections. Karl Lagerfeld designed the Sac 2005 for Chanel, in which seams and zips seem to vanish into a one-piece black leather object with metallic straps. Trussardi designed a belt that is as white as it is unadorned, and clearly inspired by military uniform.

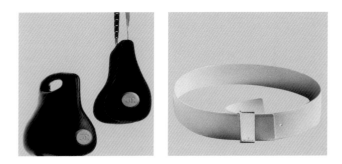

Jewelry

The minimalist tendency to eliminate everything superfluous or ornamental has not allowed jewelry-making to develop in a minimalist direction in the same way as clothing. Jewelry has always had an ostentatious connotation, incompatible with the austere and restrained spirit of minimalism. Nevertheless, a number of avant-garde designers have created accessories with pure and simple lines that allude directly to the shapes of the artistic avant-garde of the early 20th century.

Accessories (perfumes, glasses, watches...)

It is well known that, throughout the world, no more than 300 people make up the entire market for haute couture. However, the existence of these collections is justified by their essential emblematic or brand image function. Haute couture is the label under which designers market a series of products, such as perfumes, glasses, or watches, in which they try to reflect the look of their collections. Emporio Armani's *Get Together* perfume bottles are a good example of a minimalist accessory. Their smooth lines, which are concave on one bottle and convex on the other, complete each other perfectly, creating not only a physical but also an aesthetic unit, thanks to the perfect complement of the feminine and the masculine.

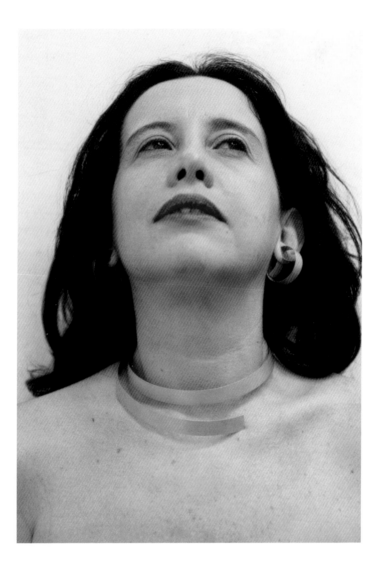

A Lifestyle for the New Millennium

Textile Development

Our appreciation of the apparent aesthetic simplicity of minimalism is accompanied today by an increasing interest in the development of new fabrics and combinations of materials. In this way fashion is catching up with industrial design, which has been dedicated to reducing the weight and volume of objects for many years. A well-known and long-standing collaboration between Makiko Minagawa and Issey Miyake aims to incorporate complex synthetic materials, like polyester and nylon, into high fashion. The German designer Jil Sander uses fabrics from the aeronautical industry in her designs, thus demonstrating her trust in technology as much as in aesthetics as a means of expression. Philippe Starck has created a garment for Wolford using no more than 7 ounces (200 grams) of stretch polyamide, which merges the sweater with a tubular, seamless one-piece dress, and is at the forefront of clothing development.

Media Popularity

Sociologists and fashion critics tend to define the end of the 20th century as an individualistic period in which, given the wide variety of aesthetic alternatives derived from different sources (ethnic, technological, deconstructive, etc.), fashion has become the result of one or more personal choices among these alternatives. However, none of the alternatives has been able to avoid the minimalist trend of the 1990s. Resulting from a process of elimination, simplification, and revision, end-of-century fashion set a standard that, despite the efforts of some designers, has succeeded in expunging the concepts of elaborate elegance and refinement in fashion.

Calvin Klein's advertising campaigns proudly proclaim "Be yourself!" over Time Square, to remind us that jeans can also be chic. By presenting Kate Moss wearing no accessories or make-up, he has transformed her into a clearly identifiable icon. At the same time he has created one of the most influential corporate images of the century, an image which is no more than the sum of a brand, a city and a model. Late 20th-century fashion is out on the streets, in the hands of marketing managers and PR companies, abandoning the concept of made-to-measure clothes and launching designs and campaigns aimed at a broader and increasingly demanding and informed public.

Minimalist Ready-to-Wear

The haute couture that survived through the 1990s has confirmed its role as the creator of emblematic collections, which influence parallel and clearly more commercial and lucrative ready-to-wear collections. Well aware of this reality, fashion houses have created such brands as Pleats Please, Emporio Armani, Calvin Klein Jeans, DKNY, and Polo. These sell basic, casual, unisex garments, sportswear, or the results of technological experimentation with the same global concept and stylistic rigor as the fashion houses that produce them, but undeniably at a price affordable to a greater number of people. Issey Miyake achieved one of the greatest commercial successes in 20th-century fashion by selling 680,000 Pleats Please garments between 1993 and 1997. The strategy is not new, and the best example of it is GAP, created in San Francisco in 1969 to market a casual look giving men, women, and children the same rights in fashion, and allowing them to buy all their clothes under one roof. This equality of rights is not lacking in glamour, and celebrities are often seen wearing these clothes, as if to say, "I'm like everyone else, I wear GAP."

Walter Chin, courtesy of GAP

Immediacy of the Retail Market

The time it takes for all the advances and achievements displayed in high-fashion collections to reach the retail market is constantly decreasing. Sometimes they are even available before the original versions are shown at the beginning of each season. Inspired by the GAP model, as described above, brands such as C&A in Germany, Next in the UK, H&M in Sweden, and Zara in Spain have no qualms about using minimalism in their collections, creating fashionable designer clothes at very low prices. This allows the minimalist style to become even more popular and available to everyone. People in the street have welcomed minimalism with open arms because the basic garments, neutral colors, and functional designs suit the urban environment. Both men and women can wear the clothes, which are equally suitable for work or going out, and for day or evening. They offer a total definitive look of refined discretion that has produced an end-of-century fashion revolution.

Pablo Soto

Pepe Botella

Design

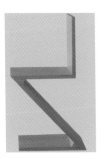  

Sofas Chairs Tables Storage Lighting Kitchens
Kitchen Accessories Bathrooms Bedrooms

Sofas

Current design trends in sofas are making legs one of their key features. The sofa body, which is usually simple in shape and strictly monochrome, seems to hover above the ground, on legs that are generally tubular and made of metal. The body itself tends to be plain and capacious, and may have a small number of cushions placed in a deliberate fashion. Armrests are either non-existent or incorporated into the structure and volume of the backrest. Fabrics are smooth and of one color, with different shades of white, sandy tones, grays, and blacks predominating. Primary colors are also used, to make the piece stand out against a neutral background.

Metropolitan sofa by Alberto Lievore,
Altherr & Molina. Made by Perobell.

Chocolate sofa by Jorge Pensi. Made by Perobell.

Batu sofa by Alberto Lievore and Jorge Pensi.
Made by Perobell.

Oberón sofa by Lievore, Altherr & Molina. Made by Perobell.

Fenice sofa by Lievore, Altherr & Molina. Made by Perobell.

Iroqua sofa by Josep Lluscà. Made by Perobell.

Metropolitan sofas by Lievore, Altherr & Molina. Made by Perobell.

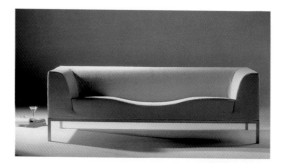

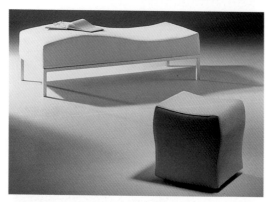

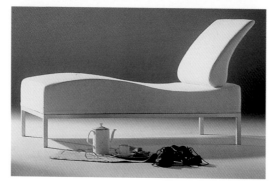

Agua collection by Diego Fortunato. Made by Perobell.

Cómodo Agua sofa by Carlos Riart.

Nit i Dia sofa bed
by Jorge Pensi.
Made by Punt Mobles.

Chairs

A strong structure and a hard-wearing finish are as important as user comfort in these chairs, which are designed to be devoid of any complex detail or seat covering (fabric or padding), with the flat surfaces and load-bearing element forming a single piece.

These objects fulfill their traditional function, but they are also made simply to lean on. They can also be stacked or folded, and are free of any additional external elements.

They are most often made of synthetic materials (plastic derivatives) with metallized finishes, or of specially treated wood laminate.

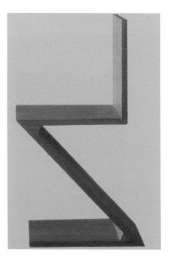

Zig Zag Stoel chair by Gerrit Rietveld (1934).

Hormiga chairs by Arne Jacobsen for Fritz Hausen.
Casa Gaspar; architect Alberto Campo Baeza.

N°. 2 chairs by Maarten van Severen.

Bulo.

Dining table and chairs by Marten
Claesson, Eero Koivisto, and Ola Rune.

Temps chair by Jorge Pensi. Made by Punt Mobles.

Austil chairs, tables, and bench by Jorge Pensi.
Made by Andrew World.

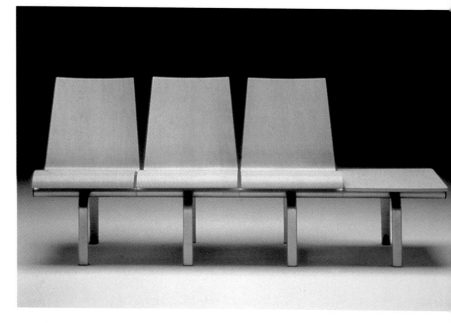

Barcino by Massana-Tremoleda. Made by Mobles 114.

Havana by Massana-Tremoleda. Made by Mobles 114.

Enea chair by Josep Lluscà. Made by Enea.

Apta chairs by Gabriel Teixidó. Made by Andrew World.

Sola chairs by Josep Lluscà. Made by Oken.

ucia chairs by Lievore, Altherr & Molina. Made by Andrew World.

Miranda chair by Dalter. Made by Andrew World.

Panton chair by Verner Panton.

Tulip chair by Eero Saarinen.

Eugeni Pons

Dining room by Eero Saarinen.
Macumba light by Örni Halloween.

Dwelling in La Azohía;
architect José Tarragó.

Tables

Here we have an extremely simple collection of furniture. Metal frameworks are generally finished in a way that enhances the material, combining harmoniously with tabletops made of wood. Straight lines, a total lack of ornamentation, and a structure as simple as it is austere are the main features of this selection.

The legs, whether of wood or metal, tend to be placed right at the corners, in such a way that the tabletop is either part of the structure itself or resting on a minimal metal frame.

La Ricarda table by A. Bonet-Equipo Santa & Cole.

Diedro table by Roberto Barbieri.

Elemental table by L. Alba and J.M. Casaponsa.

T-Square table by Moroso.

Ojalá table by Carlos Riart.

Hola y Adiós console table by Marcelo Alegre.
Made by Punt Mobles.

Mil-leni coffee table by Lola Castelló.
Made by Punt Mobles.

Mind the Gap coffee table by
El último grito. Made by Punt Mobles.

Buenavista table by Oleguer Armengol.

Molina pedestal by Jaume Sams.

Raíz Cuadrada
coffee table by Interi.

Villa Neuendorf;
architects John Pawson
and Claudio Silvestrin.

Travertine table with chairs,
by Hans J. Wegner.

Storage

Here are closets and cupboards, sideboards, shelf units, bookcases, and everything else you need to keep the house tidy.

The designs often use inconspicuous metallic legs so that the bulk of the furniture is slightly off the floor. As if wanting to preserve the unity of the floor, the legs, or in some cases wheels, raise the body and make it appear lighter.

These are simple boxes, hanging from the wall or seeming to hover above the floor, with proportions that are carefully considered. Many of the items can be disassembled for easy removal.

Light-colored wood, lacquered in neutral tones, and translucent surfaces are characteristic of this furniture.

Wood and aluminum bookcase with all-purpose, height-adjustable units. By the Belgian Maarten van Severen.

Long, low aluminum sideboard with sliding door. By Maarten van Severen.

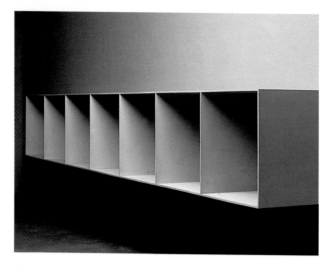

The **Magna** shelf unit by Habitat comes in two different heights and is made in natural beechwood

7V90 bookcase, designed in metal by Maarten van Severen.

The doors of this hanging storage unit close under their own weight. This very versatile item of furniture can be used to store files, office items, clothes, or kitchen utensils. By Marcus Botsch for Moormann Möbel.

The **Tria** shelf unit is fixed to the wall with ladder-shaped sides in metal.
The shelves are made of wood. Design by Massana-Tremoleda.

Bookcase by Pas/D'Urbino/Lounazzi, for Disform.

The **E1** shelf unit may be used to store anything from books to wine, even towels. By Konstantin Grcic, for Moorman Möbel.

The **Clickmore** shelving system can easily be altered and extended to suit individual tastes and needs. The joints and rods are made of aluminum, the shelves of plywood and the side panels of translucent white polypropylene. By Burkhardt Leitner constructiv, for Moorman Möbel.

No tools are needed to assemble this bookcase. An ingenious arrangement of metal tensioners gives it enough stability without the need for further support. Cardboard boxes slot in to complete the system. By Axel Kufus for Moorman Möbel.

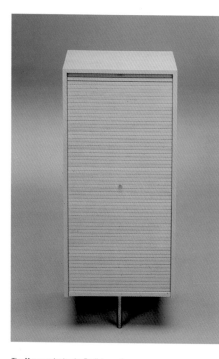

The **Home** units by the Englishman Terence
Woodgate, for Punt Mobles, are made of
natural-colored maple and cherry. Doors can
be either of translucent Plexiglass or paneled,
or made to slide up and fold away into the unit.

The units come in a range of widths.
Heights can also vary according to the model.

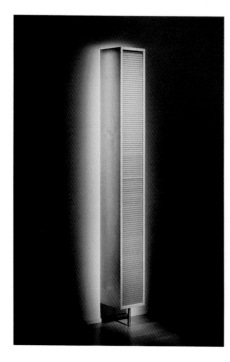

From the **Home** collection by Terence Woodgate, this slim cupboard rests on one metal leg and is fixed to the wall for stability. The door slides up and folds away inside the unit.

In this unit the doors are made of toughened glass with an aluminum frame.

Wardrobe from the **Home** collection. Made by Punt Mobles.

Wardrobe from the **Midi** system designed by Francesc Rifé
for Mobles Bellmunt. The sliding doors are of tinted glass.

This modular collection of storage units by Terence
Woodgate can be assembled in various ways, and
is finished in maple, cherry and walnut.

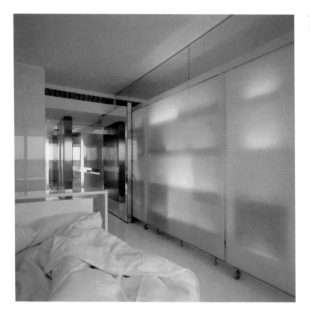

Two movable panel units designed by
Lazzarini & Pickering.

Translucent panels combine with interior
lighting in this unit from Dell'Orto

The **Frac** collection of clothes stands and hangers,
by Massana-Tremoleda, has been designed for
reception areas, offices, and bedrooms.

The **Hut ab** ("hats off") coat stand
is ideal for overcoats, bags, and
hats. It can be folded away, and
takes up virtually no space.
By Konstantin Gcric for Moorman Möbel.

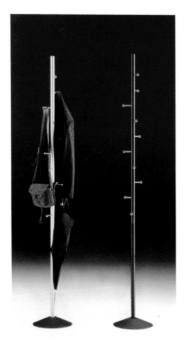

Mirac is a collection of coat racks and stands for offices, homes, and all types of reception area. Its design, which is purposely minimalist and neutral, sets aside unnecessary aesthetic considerations to create a practical, rational object. The coat stand is made up of a painted cast-iron base and an anodized aluminum pole with ten chromed brass hangers.

Riga ashtrays by Massana-Tremoleda.
Produced by Mobles 114.

Plec umbrella stands by I. Gamero/J. Pérez.
Produced by Bd Ediciones de Diseño.

Lighting

Translucent materials can diffuse light, metal panels can reflect light, small halogen spots can illuminate a single object, leaving everything else in shadow...

Some lighting is set into the architecture itself, embedded in walls or behind false ceilings. Sometimes, however, lights stand out and form part of the internal decor as objects in their own right. In the first instance the light source is almost invisible, and its purpose is to give an alternative view of the architecture, revealing different underlying aspects of an interior. In the second instance it has a role as an object, rather than a purely functional one, and the light itself can be seen just like any other piece of abstract furniture.

The type of bulb used also influences the final effect, since it can produce warm, cold, soft, or intense light.

Light from the **Nova** range. Pendant model, by J. Mirabell and M. Raventós.

vol light by Massana-Tremoleda. Made by Mobles 114.

Zentrum lights by Jorge Pensi.
Made by Grupo B. Lux.

Copenhague light by
Equipo de Santa & Cole.

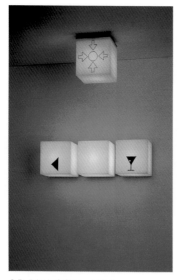

Q-Bo lights by C. Serra and J.A. Herrero.
Made by Grupo B. Lux.

Q-Bo lights by C. Serra and J.A. Herrero.
Made by Grupo B. Lux.

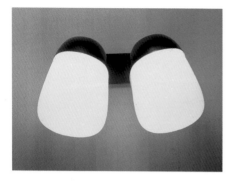

Aarlus range by A. Jacobsen and E. Moller.

Tema light by Miguel Mila.

226

Royal light by Arne Jacobsen.

Aarlus range. Pendant model, by A. Jacobsen and E. Moller.

Disco light by J. Mirabell and M. Raventós.

Nova range by J. Mirabell and M. Raventós.

Wellington range by Lluís Clotet. Made by Bd Ediciones de Diseño.

K-System light by
Laia Roca. Made by
Grupo B. Lux.

Nite light by Jorge Pensi. Made by Grupo B. Lux.

Bib semiesfera by Óscar Tusquets. Made by Bd. Ediciones de Diseño.

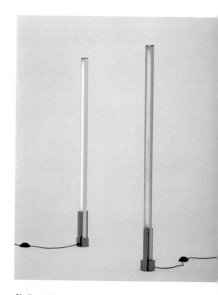

Skyline by Manuel Romagosa. Made by Bd. Ediciones de Diseño.

Flamingo light by Álvaro Siza. Made by Ediciones de Diseño.

Ebro light by Lluís Clotet. Made by Bd. Ediciones de Diseño.

Ebro light by Pepe Cortés. Made by Bd. Ediciones de Diseño.

Olvidada light by Pepe Cortés. Made by Bd. Ediciones de Diseño.

Kitchens

Over the past century, there have been remarkable and progressive changes in the character of the kitchen and in its relationship with the rest of the home. The association of the kitchen with relatively new living spaces, such as lofts, as well as its closer connection with different types of traditional kitchen such as the well-known American-style kitchen, is giving it a very important role in the world of design. The kitchen is now asserting itself, and becoming part of the living space.

Easily cleaned, hard-wearing materials, ample work surfaces and, in general, the provision of a comfortable space where freedom of movement and efficiency are combined to the full, are the features that make a kitchen comfortable, pleasant, and suited to the needs of everyday life.

The new Italian kitchen by Antonio Citterio.

Roll-top unit for storing
small electrical items.
The closing mechanism
is smooth and silent.
By Bulthaup.

Both the architecture and furniture are
inspired by Bauhaus style. Enamelled
structures, in sand and white, are combined
with aluminum. Kitchen by Bulthaup.

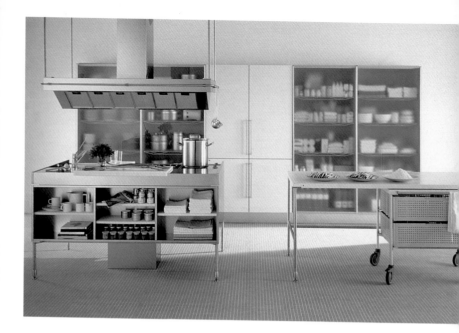

Stainless steel and translucent glass are combined in these
units from the **Archimea** collection by Antonio Citterio.

Although lines are reduced to a bare minimum, Bulthaup kitchens create an intimate and comfortable environment.

Larch and stainless steel are harmoniously combined in this arrangement. The worktops and panels highlight the horizontal and vertical lines. By Bulthaup.

Three island units and a system of peripheral cupboards are a good alternative offered by Bulthaup.

This linear arrangement is for a space dominated by a vast window. By Bulthaup.

The design of these kitchens is governed above all by principles of ergonomics and
functionality. The architecture of the available space is an essential point of departure.

The choice of materials and colors has a bearing on the effect of each object on the whole environment and, therefore, on the overall perception of the space. Inspired by minimalist aesthetics, Bulthaup creates vital spaces that convey an intimate sense of comfort.

The basic features of a kitchen – work surfaces, panels, and functional elements with their different finishes – are combined in arrangements that make the most of interacting with the space, thereby creating solutions tailored to the inhabitants of a house, whether young or old.

Kitchen of Moerkerke House
by John Pawson, London

Kitchen unit in a Majorcan *finca*, by the
architect Vincent van Duysen.

Stainless-steel kitchen in an
apartment by Simon Conder

Reiner Lautwein

Reiner Lautwein

A block of granite forms the island unit of the kitchen in this apartment, by architects Claire Bataille and Paul Ibens.

Much of the furniture in this house was made to order. House in Ibiza by architect Stéphane Bourgeois.

Pere Planells

Kitchen Accessories

Simple geometry, combining straight lines with soft curves, creates basic and well-defined shapes. Actions such as pouring, gripping, picking up, or storing are translated into clearly distinct forms within a single object.

The most commonly used materials are stainless steel, which gives kitchen utensils a long life as well as a clean appearance, brightly colored plastics, and clear glass.

In general, the objects consist of very few parts, and are manufactured entirely from the same material. This avoids having to show the joins between separate components.

The **Socrates** corkscrew by Jasper Morrison for Alessi.

The famous **Juicy Sally** lemon squeeze
by Philippe Starck (1990) for Alessi

Moka coffee maker in aluminum. The upper part is a design by Aldo Rossi for Alessi.

Diáfana kitchen uplighter by Óscar Tusquets. Made by Bd Ediciones de Diseño.

Dual-purpose solutions for different situations: this can be either a tray or a tray-table with stainless-steel base. By Jasper Morrison for Alessi.

Tria shelving by Massana-Tremoleda. The metal sides are combined with stainless-steel shelves and storage containers in the same material. Made by Mobles 114

Mami, a complete set of saucepans by Stefano Giovannoni, for Alessi. The series also includes non-stick aluminum skillets and griddle pan.

he **Bravero** porcelain dinner service by Achille Castiglione, for Alessi,
s based on the simple principle of folded-down rims.

All these pieces are reissues of designs b
Bauhaus, which were created in the school'
metal workshop between 1924 and 1930 unde
the direction of Lazló Moholy-Nag

Sugar bowl and milk jug by Marianne Branc
and Helmut Schulze (1926); tea strainer
by Otto Riettweger and Joseph Knau (1924
and tea caddy by Hans Przyrembel (1926
Made by Alessi

Designs by Marianne Brandt (Bauhaus), reissued for Alessi.

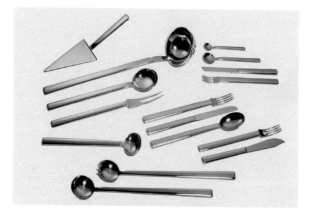

This **Rundes Modell** (1906) service produced for Alessi in 2000 is a design from the legendary Cabaret Fledermaus in Vienna, a cabaret bar and restaurant whose distinguished patrons probably included Schindler, Mahler, Schiele and even Sigmund Freud himself.

Produced in 1987 for Alessi under the guidance of Alberto Gazzi, the **Nonovo Milano** is already a classic.

Tin Family is the name given to this set of stainless-steel containers for storing salt, sugar, cereals, biscuits, and cakes. By Jasper Morrison for Alessi.

Pepe le Moko grinds sea salt and different types
of peppercorn. By Jasper Morrison for Alessi.

Salad servers for the **Twin Salad
Bowl**. By Jasper Morrison for Alessi.

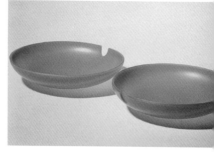

The **Twin Salad Bowl** is striking in its schematic elegance
and archetypal shape. The object is duplicated to form the lid,
and the small notch in the rim enables it to be easily opened.
By Jasper Morrison for Alessi.

The **Boaat** series includes earthenware containers for the kitchen, with lids and footed bowls. A design inspired by Japanese cuisine. By Philippe Starck for Alessi.

Bathrooms

Clean, light surfaces visually extend the space, reflect light, and are also very hygienic.

Wooden bathtubs, stone sinks, and custom-made showers are exclusive designs that reject market standardization. Thus, pieces of sanitary ware are transformed into abstract shapes to hold water or into translucent glass boxes housing showers – isolated objects set in the middle of the available space, creating new topographies that emerge from the floor and walls. A common theme in all these utility items and their accessories is their elevated status. Taps, for example, appear as objects independent of their sinks, bathtubs, or showers, as if they were pieces of stainless-steel cutlery elegantly displayed on an immense table.

Marco de Valdivia

Marco de Valdivia

Sink and bathtub by English designer John Pawson, for Villa Neuendorf in Majorca.

Bathroom of a London apartment redesigned by Simon Conder (1995).

Sink made by Rob Wellington
Quigley, at Capistrano Beach

The French designer
Philippe Starck has
created a number of
bathroom pieces,
working with
companies such as
Duravit (sanitary ware),
Hansgrohe (taps and
accessories), and
Rapsell (lavatories).

This Duravit product, with its
severe lines, is a simple white
box attached to the wall.

Bathroom of an
apartment in Vienna,
by Lichtblau & Wagner.

In the bathroom of this Majorcan *finca*, by Vincent van Duysen, the sink is a single piece cut in stone. The taps on the bathtub stand out elegantly against a white background.

Bathroom in Moerkerke House, by John Pawson. At the far end, a mirror set into the wall confuses its reflection with the white of the walls.

Each artifact takes an abstract form in this bathroom, designed by Claire Bataille and Paul Ibens. The glass shower cubicle does not interrupt the space, and the bathtub is simply a slab of stone that keeps the water in one corner.

This bathroom is in a minimalist apartment overlooking the Thames, by John Pawson.

Richard Glover

In this house in Ibiza, Stéphane Bourgeois has created a bathroom that is part of the bedroom. Bathtub, sinks, and shower were all made to order.

Pere Planells

Ross Honeysett

The combination of mirrored walls and glass screens
stretching from floor to ceiling creates an interesting
effect. The whole bathroom is reflected in the far wall,
making it look twice its size.

In the bathroom of the Huete house by Spanish designers Vicens and Ramos, the bathtub is sunk into the floor and the shower is behind a translucent glass screen, which defines its shape. The dark-colored cylinders of the two sinks stand out in the room.

Eugeni Pons

Eugeni Pons

Bedrooms

Mobles Bellmunt, Rifé and Associates

The **Midi** system by Mobles Bellmunt, designed by Francesc Rifé and Associates, was conceived from the strictest principles of austerity. It includes three wardrobes and three beds.

The furniture has an anodized aluminum framework of lightweight construction. The headboard and nightstands form part of an integrated unit.

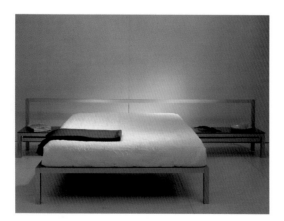

The headboard on this bed is a length of sand-colored, lacquered chipboard, with built-in lighting.

Bed system 01. Frame and headboard are formed by a hollow structure of anodized aluminum with integral nightstands. The closets have folding doors, which are finished in a sand color and outlined in aluminum to match the handles.

Bed system 02. Frame and headboard are of anodized aluminum. Headboard and integral nightstands are in bleached coigue wood. The closets have sliding doors in the same wood finish.

Bed system 03. The headboard is covered in wenge wood over a structural framework of aluminum. The nightstands are separate. The closets have sliding doors in the same wood, and aluminum handles.

Lazzarini & Pickering for Dormusa

The pieces in this ensemble consist basically of planks of wood joined at the margins. The set of tables of different sizes can be combined in various ways, with one another or with the bed, to create a working environment.

The different heights of the tables can be arranged with the bed to provide a headrest, a breakfast tray, or somewhere to leave clothes at the foot of the bed.

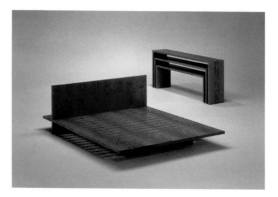

Sofa, bed, and table.

This series of tables can be arranged in a number of ways.

Single bed and tables.

This bed, in an apartment designed by Simon Conder, is made from a single length of wood that has been cut to form the headboard.

Richard Glover

Eugeni Pons

Bedroom of an apartment in Barcelona, by Bercedo + Mestre.

The bedroom of Moerkerke House, by architect John Pawson, contains only this simple wooden bed in the same tone as the floor.

Richard Glover

Architecture

Photo: Juan Purcell

Photo: Ruedi Walti

Photo: H. Helfenstein

Hakuei House | Akira Sakamoto

This site is flanked by two streets, one of which intersects a third one. Passersby can see through the building to a small wooded area on the other side, which makes the house airy and permeable.

The basic design idea was to represent the outside inside, and vice versa, and thus to create a continuous space between the two environments.

A wall guides your eye from one street to the other, while the house consists of three white boxes facing one another, two of them symmetrical. Two discontinuous walls with openings traverse the space, giving a sense of fluidity and continuity. Movement among the inhabitants of the house behind the walls can be guessed at, and links are therefore created between the boundaries and the internal and external spaces. Each room is accessed in a different way and has different visual relations. All the rooms are also lit in various ways, using skylights, continuous windows, or small openings in the corners.

This kind of architecture encourages silence and reflection, guiding your thoughts and your eyes to the smallest things, which in other environments would be hidden by clutter.

Architect: Akira Sakamoto
Location: Osaka, Japan
Photography: Nacása & Partners

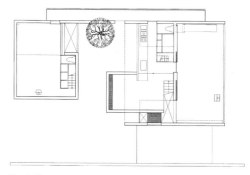

First floor

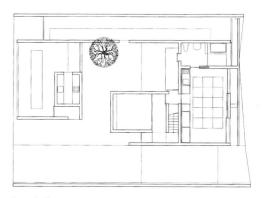

Ground floor

The finish on the walls around the patio is the same as that in the interior.
This reinforces
the idea of a
relationship
and continuity
between the
inside and the
outside of the
building. The
tree is the only
element on the
patio, representing
a synthesis of the
cycles of nature,
living beings, and time.

House without Walls | Shigeru Ban

This pavilion is part of a series of experimental designs that the architect has called Case Study Houses. Built on a slope to keep excavation work to a minimum, the house looks as if its back half has been buried in the ground. The floor curves at one end to join the roof, which is supported only by three very slim, round pillars. The basic design concept was to achieve the same spatial continuity inside as outside. Two planes, denoted by the floor and the roof, demarcate and define a horizon. All boundaries have been eliminated, the internal space has no divisions, and there is total visibility, even in the more private areas like the bathroom, which is brutally open to view. Only the kitchen units, a bench, and a few pieces of furniture suggest small differences between areas in this single, smooth, and uniform space.

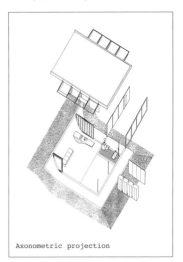

Axonometric projection

The house has multiple uses, and can be transformed by the use of sliding panels to give each room its own character. The curvilinear shapes are extremely simple, the structure almost disappears, and the complete transparency of the outer limits means that the house is contained within its landscape.

Architect: Shigeru Ban

Location: Nagano, Japan

Photography: Hiroyuki Hirai

Design concepts
have been taken
to extremes in
the design of
this house,
to the point of interfering with its function.

Becky's Birthday | Rothenberry + Wellen

The clients own a ranch in western Texas, and needed a cabin for guests to stay in. Alternatively, it would also be used as a meeting place for ranch business and to entertain large groups of people.

They asked for it to include a covered parking area, a basic kitchen, a bathroom, and a sleeping area. The project was carried out by renovating part of an existing but semi-demolished ranch building surrounded by a line of trees.

A building was designed with sliding doors and windows that could provide relief from the extreme temperatures of the Texas climate. The sleeping area is over the kitchen, and the bathroom is next to some high windows for good ventilation. Modular panels can be drawn for protection against insects.

This sensible structure differs greatly from the sometimes romantic shapes and materials normally associated with rural architecture in Texas, favoring a pre-designed structure with a corrugated, galvanized steel roof and walls. The simple shapes of door and window frames are common in the region, allowing buildings to be put up quickly and inexpensively in remote places like this one.

Architects: Rothenberry + Wellen
Location: Texas, USA
Photography: Hester + Hardaway

The raw look of the structure contrasts with the stone of the fireplace, which was made from recycled materials recovered from abandoned buildings near the ranch where the client grew up. The sensitive reuse of materials provides continuity in the building of new structures, and reflects the practical mentality of these ranchers.

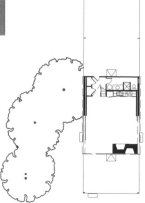

Ground floor

Villa in the Woods | Kazuyo Sejima

This villa in the woods of Tateshina provides shelter from the immensity of the outside world, a place of authenticity in the midst of chaos. Kazuyo Sejima has chosen a circular structure to reflect the feeling of uniformity created by wood. The wooded surroundings have no center, and the sun's rays filtered through the branches make it difficult to find your way.

The client, a Tokyo art gallery owner, wanted a house that would serve as a second home with an exhibition area, and where he could entertain guests. The design follows a central circular space where the architect has placed the rooms that perform the essential functions of the home.

This arrangement makes it easy to move around, both inside and outside the building, demonstrating that architecture is mobility. The container, in which movement is predetermined, produces an inevitable effect of emptiness. We can think of the house as being built around a luminous empty space, which can be accessed visually or physically through a number of specific openings. As with any plan for a new house, the dream was to build a new body that would transform the spirit.

Architect: Kazuyo Sejima
Location: Nagano, Japan
Photography: Nacása & Partners

Sejima believes that design is all about shapes. Architecture is the creation of shapes, which are suggested by the purpose to be fulfilled, and then interact with their surroundings.

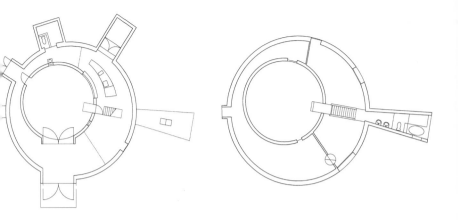

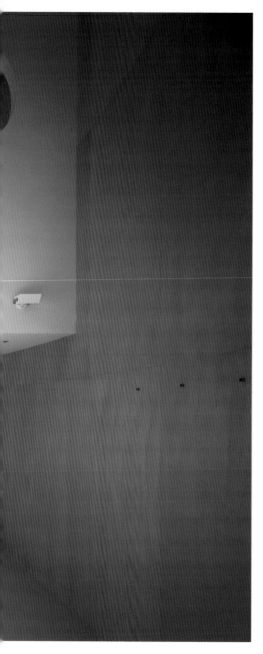

House S | Toyo Ito

The clients of House S are an artist couple, who required a studio and exhibition room in addition to domestic areas. They wanted many of their work-related activities to be fully visible to neighbors and curious people who might approach the house. Their home and studio also had to allow for conversion into a cultural center that they could use to show their work. They therefore agreed with the architect's view that the various areas of the house should have a direct relationship with the exterior.

The home stands on the edge of an artificial pond (built as an irrigation reservoir) and close to a mountainside. It makes no attempt to integrate with the landscape, change the topography, or adapt to the slope. It is built on an artificial rectangular, perfectly flat platform, just as it could be anywhere else.

The structure consists of two rows of pillars supporting a corrugated sheet-metal roof measuring 100 x 20 feet (30 x 6 meters). Under the roof are alternating open and closed spaces. The general image is that of a pergola under which a number of containers have been placed.

Architect: Toyo Ito

Location: Ogumi, Japan

Photography: Nacása & Partners

The spaces are enclosed using prefabricated elements and unclad materials. In addition to the metal structure, there are elements of bare concrete and glass (both transparent and translucent). There is no color other than gray.

Häusler House | Baumschlager & Eberle

Häusler House is a detached home in Hard, Austria, built on a flat, open piece of land. Its strictly geometrical shape contrasts with the almost uninterrupted landscape, where a number of buildings stand in no pre-established order.

The house has been purposely designed to be different from the surrounding buildings, most of which are architecturally bland detached homes with gabled roofs, few differences between them and no clear relationship with the surrounding landscape.

Häusler House, however, has an emphatic, conceptual and well-defined shape. It consists essentially of a rectangular container, devoid of any cladding in order to display its gray concrete texture. The internal design is the result of gradually subtracting areas from the initial rectangle. These are converted into the terrace and other light and airy spaces, which form the various rooms of the house. The subtraction of areas allows an interesting relationship between the outside and the inside of the building, while ensuring that the internal areas remain sufficiently light and spacious.

Architects: Baumschlager & Eberle
Location: Hard, Austria
Photography: Eduard Hueber

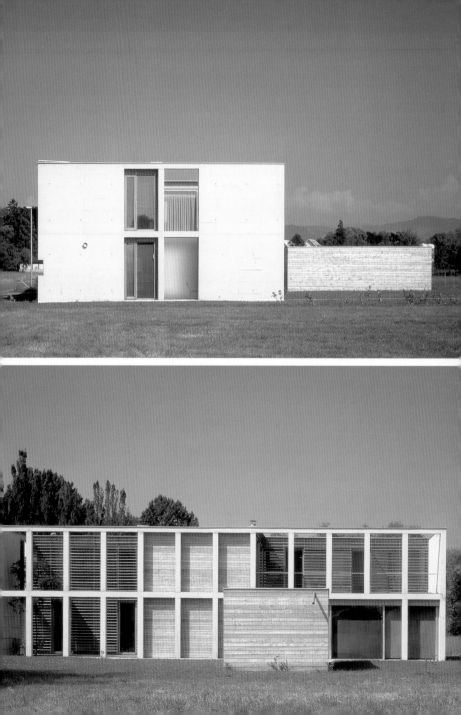

The front and sides
of the building are
practically closed
off; only the southern
side is completely open.
This facade is in the
form of a concrete
grid, behind which
different slatted
wood-laminate partitions
can be seen, positioned at various distances from the edge of the building.

The northern (access)
side is a gray concrete
rectangle with just two
openings, the front door
and a long, narrow,
horizontal window. The
great contrast between
the two facades clearly
distinguishes the front
from the back, the first
being open, the second closed, as dictated by their orientation.

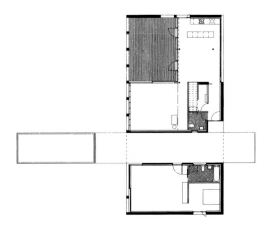

Ground floor

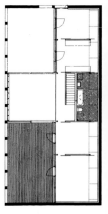

Upper floor

Leisure-Time Studio | Group J. Kaakko, I. Laine, K. Liimatainen, J. Tirkkonen

This leisure-time studio stands in a landscaped area of Puolarmaari, in Espoo, Finland. The group of designers rented the land for the experimental building in 1991, and the structure was exhibited at the leisure buildings construction exhibition in June 1992.

Conceived by a group of four young architects, the design was borne of an urgency to see plans put into practice. One of the driving forces was the architects' desire to influence the result as much as possible, to the point that they actually built it with their own hands. Assistance and permissions given by building companies made the project financially viable, and meant that the group only had half of the overall costs to cover.

The building is a flexible and versatile living and working environment, a place where artists from different fields can spend their free time or work together. It is equipped with a sauna with a see through roof, allowing daylight to filter through.

The whole assembly was designed as a dark, heavy mass within a light, transparent structure. The facilities are all together in a cohesive unit within the dark block, which is surrounded by an open workspace directly linked to the exterior.

Architects: Group J. Kaakko, I Laine,
K. Liimatainen, J. Tirkkonen
Location: Espoo, Finland
Photography: Jussi Tiainen

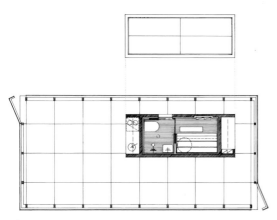

Floor plan

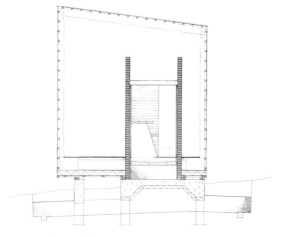

Cross section

As the studio has no heating, it cannot be used in winter. In summer the heat is tempered by the shade from the trees and good ventilation. The mass of dark stone also helps to regulate external temperatures. The studio attracted a great deal of attention when it was shown at the leisure buildings exhibition, and was both highly praised and strongly criticized. Perhaps that is what makes it so special.

Villa M | Stéphane Beel

The site occupied by Villa M is a clearing in a wood, occupying a completely flat area of about 2.5 acres (1 hectare) in the garden of a nearby mansion, from which it is separated by brick walls. As Beel explains, the absence of explicit restrictions or boundaries on the site is perhaps the only (implicit) limitation: "It demonstrates the intention of doing almost nothing: an elementary gesture which, in its simplicity, will consolidate rather than interfere."

The result is an extremely large dwelling measuring 200 x 23 feet (60 x 7 meters), running parallel to one of the existing walls. Walls are a familiar feature of the garden, but this is one wall within which you can live.

The various areas are arranged along the length of the house in sequence, separated by silent architectural spaces. Some are small patios and others are sectioned-off areas for facilities. The function of these silent spaces is to distance adjoining rooms from one another. This means that, despite the absence of doors to interrupt the spatial continuity, rooms can be separated.

The bedrooms are at the two ends of the building. The children's are on the north side, connected by a wide corridor that doubles as a playroom, while the main bedroom is on the south side.

Architect: Stéphane Beel
Location: Zedelgem, Belgium
Photography: Lieve Blancquart

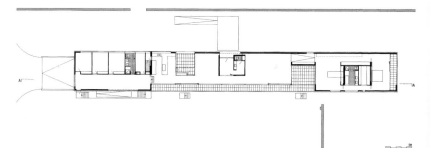

Ground floor

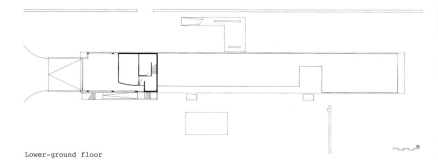

Lower-ground floor

From the garden,
as night falls,
the inside of
the house looks
like a stage
set. Through the
enormous glass
openings, people
moving inside
can be followed
around the rooms
as if they were
characters in a
dumb show, standing
on a wooden dais. From
inside, the great
expanses of glass
frame the landscape like pictures, disturbed only by leaves blowing in the wind.

Klotz House | Mathias Klotz

Klotz House stands on a site near Tongoy, a beach about 250 miles (400 kilometers) from Santiago, Chile. It is a 15-mile (24-kilometer) bay with very few buildings around it. From a distance you can see the contour of the bay and the mountains behind it. The house contrasts markedly with its environment. It is a rectangular prism measuring 20 x 20 x 40 feet (6 x 6 x 12 meters), that seems to rest on the ground almost without touching it. Externally, it has a windowless side, accessed from a curved bridge. The other side looks out to sea and has large windows.

Inside, partitions divide the space into two very different areas: on one side the entrance, bathrooms, and one small bedroom; and on the other the main bedroom, a kitchen-diner, and a double-height sitting room. On the second floor, bedrooms are arranged along the windowless side to make room for terraces, the staircase, and the bridge between them. The fine carpentry, the color white, the wall openings, the attached and separate elements, the play of proportions, and the horizontal lines of the wooden flashings on the facades all emphasize the proximity of everything. This is in contrast with the wide, open spaces surrounding the building and the abstract nature of the structure.

Architect: Mathias Klotz

Location: Playa Grande, Tongoy, Chile

Photography: Juan Purcell

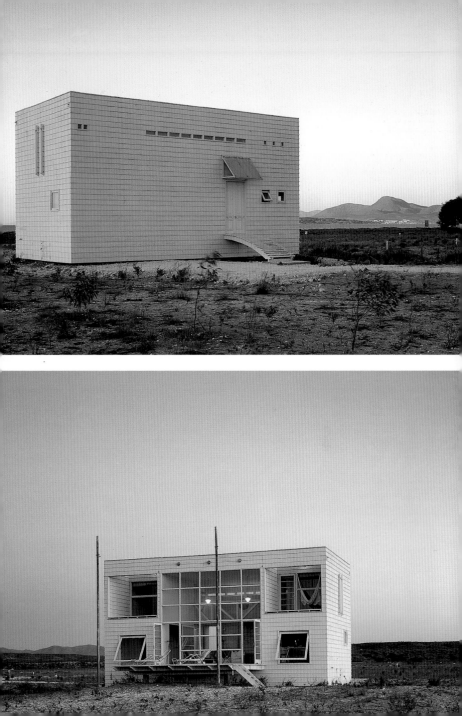

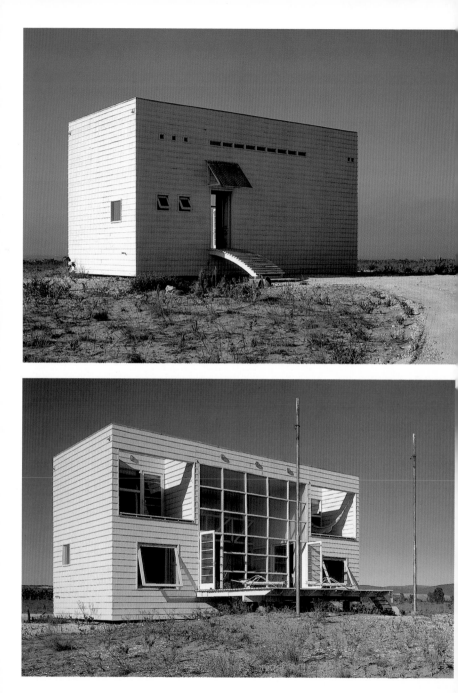

The whiteness, the fine carpentry, and the openings in the walls that allow natural light to shine through, as well as the play of proportions and horizontal lines, define the minimalist aesthetics of Klotz House.

Lakeside Cabin | Isabelle Poulain

This building stands on the edge of a lake surrounded by woods. Houses are forbidden on this land, so the French architect, who owns the site, decided to build this wooden cabin. The structure is a box that is open and closed at the same time. Not really a house, because it has no running water or electricity, it is made of recycled materials and is more like a hut, a shelter, or a terrace at the edge of a pond.

The terrace is 8 feet (2.5 meters) from the ground and supported by old telegraph poles. The walls have been treated as screens and are independent of one another. They consist of the wooden panels used to make shuttering for concrete structures.

You can choose between having a terrace of 750 square feet (70 square meters) or a house of 320 square feet (30 square meters). The metamorphosis is made possible by cables, which lift the whole west-facing side of the cabin inward. The roof is made of corrugated steel, painted green and the wooden panels have simply been coated with a light-colored varnish. A bench and handrail surround the platform and, inside, two rectangular items of furniture complement the symmetry of the building as a whole.

Architect: Isabelle Poulain

Location: Indre-et-Loire, France

Photography: Image de Marc

This cabin or
shelter stands
on a 750 square-foot
(70 square-meter)
platform made of
Oregon pine, which
was previously
waterproofed and
treated with a
protective coating against insects.

343

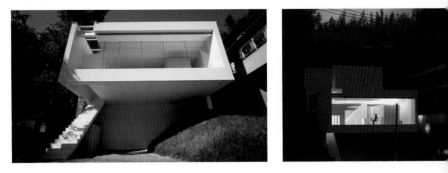

House in Dazaifu | Hiroyuki Arima

Hiroyuki Arima has created a dwelling that makes the most of the landscape and the light. The value of the building lies in the way it includes nature, rather than in its functional efficiency or effectiveness.

This is an extreme design, which attempts to create a connection between the inside and the outside, a visual but real relationship. Nature is incorporated into the home by appropriating its characteristics: indoor plants, natural ventilation, and daylight. The aim of the design is to create spaces to be enjoyed by the senses.

The house is divided into two blocks on different levels, situated on a slope measuring about 30 feet (10 meters) from top to bottom. The blocks are independent of each another, but linked by a path running down the steepest side of the site.

On the lower level, occupants can admire different views of the mountains of Dazaifu. This floor, where visual awareness is the most important thing, consists of a room containing boxes acting as functional units: kitchen, living space, and bathroom.

Upstairs, the external boundaries are much more clearly defined: there is a living room which can be modified by moving mobile partitions, and a walled garden.

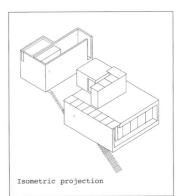

Isometric projection

Architect: Hiroyuki Arima

Location: Dazaifu, Japan

Photography: Koji Okamoto

The staircases have been meticulously designed: from each step you have a direct view of the sky, while the steps in the upper part of the house are translucent, to allow light to shine through them from above.

House in Lochau | Baumschlager & Eberle

Carlo Baumschlager and Dietmar Eberle focus on the creative process when making buildings, communicating with clients to find solutions that satisfy their requirements, producing structures in harmony with their environment, and considering the needs of the various professionals involved in construction. All these elements converge to create a sensitive, functional, and distinguished kind of architecture.

The house in Lochau is a good example of this style. It stands on a huge plot of land belonging to the client's family. The client was particularly concerned to ensure that no other buildings would spoil the magnificent views of the nearby lake.

The design has a simple but practical layout. The lower floor houses the garage – which also acts as a space for domestic and professional activities – as well as various other fixtures and a bathroom, allowing this floor to be used by guests.

The upper floor houses the living room and bedrooms, while the kitchen and bathroom are in an annex. This floor is intended to be all one space, with different areas flowing into one another with no apparent physical partitions. Having a separate kitchen and bathroom ensures that there are no obstacles in the relaxation areas, which have the best views.

Architects: Baumschlager & Eberle
Location: Lochau, Austria
Photography: Eduard Hueber

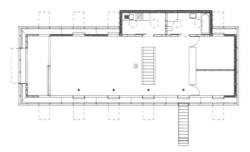

Upper floor

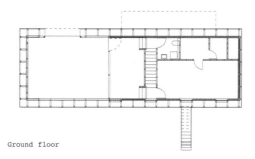

Ground floor

The double facade is one of the most interesting concepts of the design. It is dictated by the advantages inherent in prefabricating certain building elements, both to make construction easier and to keep costs down, and by the need to establish a relationship between the building and the surrounding space.

Dayton House | Vincent James Associates

Situated in the suburbs of Minneapolis, next to a lake and surrounded by a sculpture garden this house is based on the idea of a pavilion. It very simple shape consists of a combination of full and empty spaces. The rigidity of the building dissolves when the glazed partitions slide back into the thick walls, allowing the breeze from the lake to blow through the house.

The walls surrounding the plot have been kept low, to allow neighbors to keep their pleasant view of the lake and now of the sculpture garden.

The outer walls convey power and authority, and are given great importance in the design. They house the structure and installations, the chimney, and the sliding doors.

The originality of this disciplined and multifunctional home – pavilion, art gallery, observatory – lies in the fact that, despite the complex agenda and the restricted size of the plot, it provides visual serenity, both inside the home and from the garden. The architectural rigor does not in any way detract from the lightness of the building.

Architects: Vincent James Associates
Location: Minneapolis, USA
Photography: Don F. Wong

The landscaper Georges Hardgraves designed the garden, and the artist
James Carpenter
oversaw the glazing.
To reach the entrance,
the visitor walks
along a path
through the
sculpture garden.

The space inside is
fluid, with open views
of the garden and
lake in a number
of directions. The
garden seems to
merge into the living room, which seems like an extension of the exterior.

357

House P | Pauhof Architects

This detached house is in the Austrian countryside, among rolling fields dotted with trees and gentle hills in the background.

The house is essentially one mass divided into two blocks. The first one, covered with sheet aluminum, is polished and ethereal, and seems to hover above the second, larger and heavier one made of bare concrete. The two blocks have a conventional residential layout, with the first housing the bedrooms and the second the sitting rooms and utilities. The former has rooms facing east and west and the latter is south-facing. This play of opposites is the defining feature of a design that rejects the typological and semantic stereotypes of rural Austrian architecture.

The choice of materials, the clever way in which the links are controlled, the textures, the details, and the openness of the interior to the outside world are the major achievements of this house.

The two blocks combine with one another without touching. The metallic box rests on a central pillar and on a staircase wall. Similarly, the lower box is raised slightly above the ground, to allow light to shine through a narrow opening along the baseboards.

Architects: Pauhof Architects

Location: Gramastetten, Austria

Photography: Matteo Piazza

There appears to be no contact between the two elements. Interior walls of
reinforced concrete
and a pillar support
the metal house,
which does not touch
the ground. The wall
of the access facade
is extended, to give
the garden privacy
and to form a pergola.

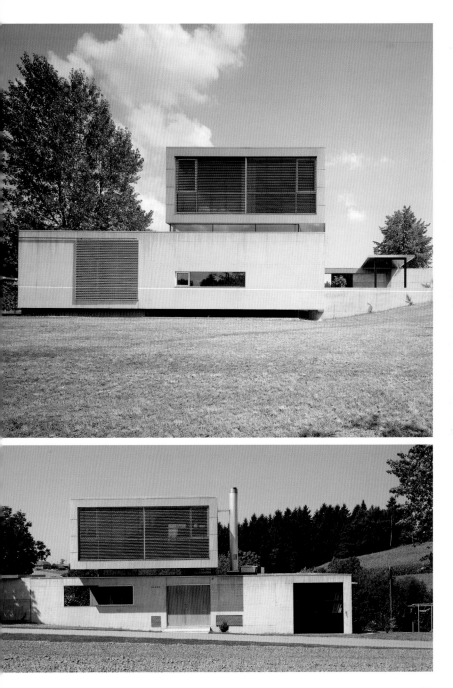

In contrast to the sobriety of the facades, the interior of the house is warm and welcoming, with materials and textures carefully selected to heighten this effect. The way in which the upper section rests on the lower, without touching it, allows light to enter all parts of the ground floor.

Sperl House | Adolf Krischanitz

This plot of land is in Zurndorf-Friedrichshof, east of Vienna, Austria. The building was designed as part of a general scheme to develop the area, which included a total of 150 homes built on long, narrow plots of land, occasionally forming large, independent housing complexes. The resulting arrangement of buildings is generally in line with the tradition of building at the front of the plot of land.

The general scheme for the area was to create a large natural space at the center of the planned building lots, which measured 25 feet (7.5 meters) by between 200 and 500 feet (60 and 150 meters), to ensure high density without requiring excessively large amounts of land. This was achieved by adopting the extended patio design typical of the region, which allows the land to be simply divided into narrow, deep lots.

By strictly employing this existing type of design and using current technical advances, a type of architecture was developed based on quite long but narrow-fronted buildings, creating a systematic series of distinct units that can be extended to suit individual preferences and tastes.

Architect: Adolf Krischanitz

Location: Vienna, Austria

Photography: Margherita Spiluttini, Chris Pfaff

The architecture of this house consists of a series of bi-directional partitions, some of them structural and others purely to divide up the space. Given the length of the plot and the narrowness of the facades, a determined effort had to be made to design points of entry for natural light.

Low-Cost Housing in Graz | Riegler Riewe

The conditions set for this low-cost project were not very specific. The work was commissioned directly by the client, and there were neither any aesthetic requirements nor any need to intervene during the design process to listen to the contributions of future tenants.

The character of the building is severe in terms of shape and materials, both of which are entirely suited to its location in a peaceful, semi-urban area of the suburbs of Graz, in Austria.

The facade consists of prefabricated concrete slabs with windows fitted between them. Sliding panels of galvanized-metal mesh offer privacy, and shield occupants from the sun. These panels form a mobile system that acts as the counterpoint to this rigid and static facade, which is devoid of ornamentation.

For two reasons, a deliberate effort was made not to create a relationship between the building and its surroundings, for example by adding balconies or small gardens. Firstly, the intention was to give all the floors the same features, and secondly, given the location of the apartment building in a relatively green environment, there was no need to create individual gardens.

Architects: Riegler Riewe
Location: Graz, Austria
Photography: Paul Ott

The combination of sliding panels and concrete slabs forms an arrangement that changes constantly according to whether the panels are being used. The contrasting full and empty spaces play with the semi-transparency of the metallic blinds. Concrete, metal, and glass leave no room for decorative elements.

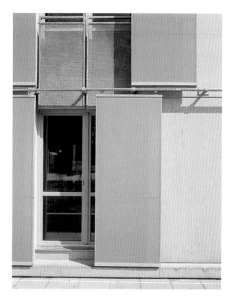

HT96.4 | Angélil/Graham/Pfenninger/Scholl Architecture

This building, on a hill overlooking a lake, consists of two dwellings arranged one on top of the other, and measuring around 5,400 square feet (500 square meters) in total. Both have been built using prefabricated panels: wooden ones for the upper section and concrete ones for the lower one.

The two homes have a similar floor area but are divided up differently. The roof of the wooden house slopes lengthwise to make room for a partition and crosswise to increase the surface area of the facade and gain sunlight. Windows are either horizontal and sliding, or full-height. Internal spaces have been arranged in such a way as to make the most of the lake views and receive sunlight from the south. Kitchens and bathrooms have been arranged as individual islands intersecting the space.

The neutral areas of the concrete house, on the lower floor, have been designed to be interchangeable. The patio is split into four areas, which have been paved in different materials to produce a height difference of 20 inches (50 centimeters) between each area. While the internal spaces are perfectly rectangular in plan, variations in the height of the roof serve to differentiate them.

Architects: Angélil/Graham/Pfenninger/
Scholl Architecture
Location: Horgen, Switzerland
Photography: Reinhard Zimmermann

To emphasize the independence of the two parts of the building,
a gap runs the entire
length of it. The
resulting effect is
that of one house
floating above the
other, allowing
daylight to shine
into the concrete house.

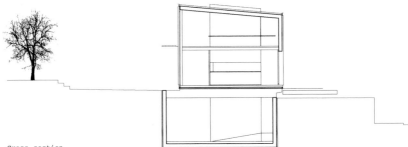

Cross section

House in Viana do Castelo | João Alvaro Rocha

Standing on a low plinth, this building is a simple, rectangular, one-story construction, with a lower-ground floor in the center. The plinth, roof and side walls form a rectangular shape over looking the sea. All the rooms can be opened to the outside, thanks to a system of wooden shutters which, when closed, are flush with the external paneling made of the same material.

Even though the house is set within this gigantic and simple frame, there is complexity in its internal areas, which combine and differ from one another according to the amount of daylight they allow in and the varying height of the ceilings. Some areas with no specific purpose, such as the porch or the lobby, are so transparent as to make the other end of the building visible. The areas are arranged in linear fashion on the longer side of the frame leaving the bathrooms on the inside.

The use of color, the mobility of the rear facade, and the subtle differences in level of the ground, lower ground floor, and main platform confer flexibility and freedom to this apparently rigid and authoritarian structure.

People constantly remark on the building's similarity to a window, perhaps because of the strength of the structure, which is born of the emphatic simplicity of its architecture.

Architect: João Alvaro Rocha
Location: Viana do Castelo, Portugal
Photography: Hélène Binet, Luis Ferreira Alves

The volumes of the
rooms extend beyond
the main body of the
building, thus creating
entry points for daylight.
Interior finishes combine
stone surfaces, wooden
floors, and partitions with smooth plastering on ceilings and walls.

Barn Conversion | Artec

This conversion and extension were carried out for a farmer and philologist who needed a space in which to work, write, and read, separate from the agricultural environment of the site. The conversion also had to include a bathroom and heating system. The basis for the design was an existing stable building, the roof of which had to be replaced to avoid the risk of collapse. Some of the new facilities were housed in the old building, which serves as a plinth for the new object added above it. This arrangement allowed the new area to be used as a suitably private reading room.

In front of the reading room there are two terraces accessed through sliding doors, which extend the internal space outward. They are typically urban elements, placed in a rural environment.

From the outside, the staircase is a component that juts out of the building, supporting itself against the wall to connect the new object with the ground. This gleaming metallic "parasite" is completely covered in smooth aluminum, and paneled with plywood on the inside.

The old building contains the bathroom, which is lit by a long, narrow skylight constructed so that it stores a layer of water on its glazed surface whenever it rains.

Architects: Artec

Location: Raum Zita, Raasdorf, Austria

Photography: Margherita Spiluttini

Stairs built against external
walls are a feature of rural
buildings in the region.
In this case, where
the stable has been
converted into living
space, the staircase
has been covered over,
becoming an internal
feature protected by a
gleaming shell. The
new attachment sits
atop the old building, twisting and molding itself to it.

The shiny smoothness of the metal contrasts starkly with
the rugged, irregular,
opaque stone, which
was not altered
in any way.

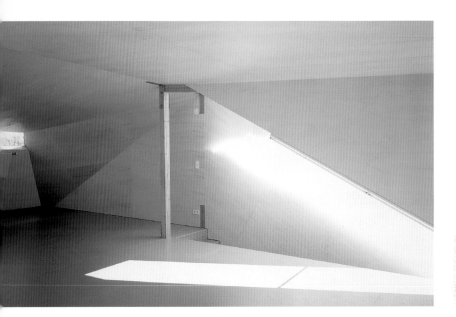

A long, narrow
skylight lights the
bathroom in the pre-existing building.

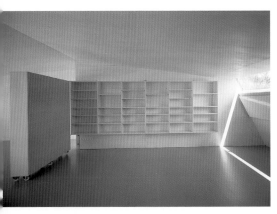

Home in La Azohía | José Tarragó

At first sight, the individuality of this house seems to lie in the monochrome color of all its elements, but what really makes it distinctive is the ambiguity of the spaces in terms of their location. The internal spaces are completely open to view, related to one another, and open to the exterior, allowing no introspection. Similarly, the patios are designed to look like interior spaces, and are encircled by walls isolating them from the surrounding landscape.

Externally, the building incorporates traditional architectural features to cope with the rigors of the climate: thick walls providing thermal insulation, whitewashing to reflect the sun's rays, and small openings preferably in the shade. The interior, however (which includes the patios), has a contemporary and almost futuristic look. The furniture combines white with multiple ochre tones and includes exclusively designed pieces. Open to the living room, the kitchen is characterized by pure lines, formal containment and the immaculate white, smooth surfaces of the cupboards.

Architect: José Tarragó

Location: Murcia, Spain

Photography: Eugeni Pons

Everything inside the house, including the furniture, is white. Protected from the exterior by high walls, the seating areas of the patios have white surfaces, which make them look like small islands taken from indoors and placed in the open air.

House Y | Katsufumi Kubota

This building stands in a distinctly residential suburb of the city of Iwakuni, in Japan. Kubota aims to distance himself from such categories as baroque or post-modern architecture, both of which attribute a concept and style to every component. In this building he has created a truly abstract space, devoid of all redundant elements.

The purpose was to create pure and transparent environments, which would establish a connection between man and his surroundings and allow people to experiment with the spaces, casting aside the prejudices and tensions of modern society to re-examine and rediscover themselves. The intention was to achieve these aims by providing a plain and simple solution containing as few elements as possible, and considering the characteristics of the area, such as the movement of light and air.

The white box opens onto the cliff and allows light breezes to blow through it, softening the sun's powerful rays. The U-shaped section of the building facing the street consists of a floor that subtly raises the space, a roof providing protection and a wall that closes it off. These extremely simple elements satisfy the requirements of the site, and combine to create an abstract space in which nothing is predetermined.

Architect: Katsufumi Kubota

Location: Iwakuni, Yamaguchi, Japan

Photography: N. Nakagawa

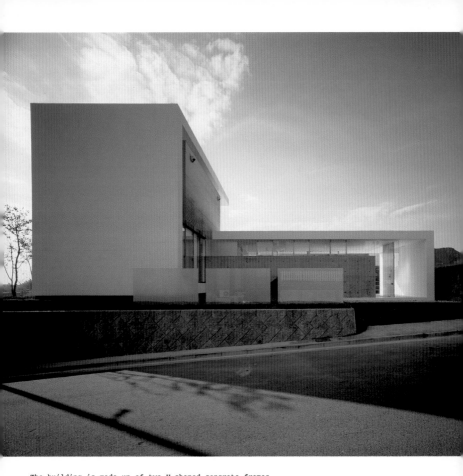

The building is made up of two U-shaped concrete frames
that combine to
create environments
in which transparency
is crucial. The house
is an airy space that
is at the same time
flexible.

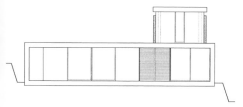

Longitudinal section

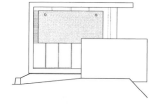

Cross section

Nirvana House | Jordi Casadevall

Nirvana House successfully establishes a dialog with the surrounding landscape. The stone-clad lower floor of the house is a strict parallelepiped 130 feet (40 meters) long. On this plinth stand two metallic cubes, which house the more private rooms and form a large shelter overhanging the exterior space.

Their disconnection from the base and the intentional contrast of materials and color between the two elements emphasize their respective properties. The solidity and rigidity of the plinth is therefore highlighted by the existence of the pavilions, which bring lightness and movement to the whole.

The entrances to the house are on the northern side of the lower floor, with separate vehicular access. Timber seems to be associated with these entrances, especially the main one, and is the only element added to the stone-clad plinth. The numerous entrances avoid excessive movements around the interior, ensuring the tranquillity and autonomy of the various areas.

Architect: Jordi Casadevall

Location: Valldoreix, Barcelona, Spain

Photography: Jordi Miralles

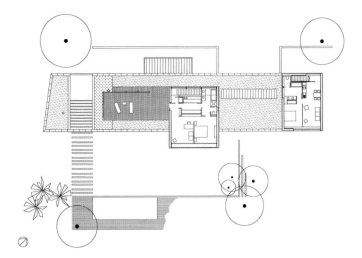

Upper floor

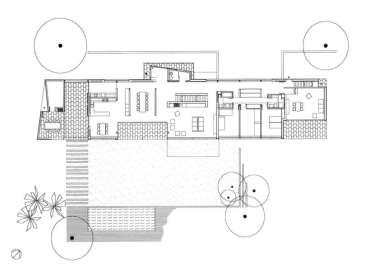

Ground floor

Nirvana is a clear example of a house where the fluidity of the internal space is not at odds with the autonomy of its different parts. The two interior staircases, which can be reached almost directly from the outside, are a good illustration of this. A firm link is therefore established between the pavilions and the rest of the house and garage, without detracting from their privacy.

The facades faithfully reflect what goes on inside and outside the house.

The Jordi Cantarell House | Eugènia Jubert and Lluís Santacana

Jordi Cantarell's house consists of a small living space and a vast exhibition room for painted furniture. The site is slightly sloping, has good views, and a pleasant position on the outskirts of a picturesque Catalan village.

The site was modified by lowering the center of the land below the entrance level, in order to create two horizontal surfaces. One of these is a garden at the same level as the entrance, and the other is an enclosed sunken patio overlooked by the main living space through a number of enormous windows. The patio has views of Púbol Castle.

Projecting from the north side of the building is a simple white shape containing the exhibition room. Below this, all the living space opens out onto the sunken patio. A staircase and ramp provide separate access to the house and exhibition room. East of the patio there is a small annex containing another room and a bathroom.

Jubert and Santacana have designed a multi-functional space characterized by aesthetic and compositional sophistication. These features were recognized when the two architects were awarded the FAD prize for architecture.

Architects: Eugènia Jubert and Lluís Santacana
Location: Púbol, Spain
Photography: Eugeni Pons and Jordi Bernadó

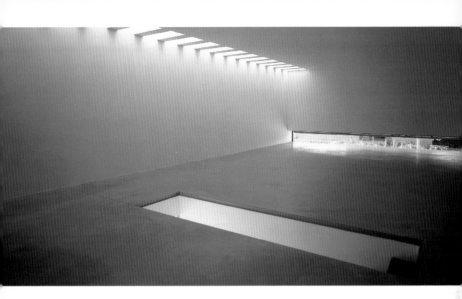

The building defines its own landscape, making the most of the views from the house across the patio, which simultaneously contains, encloses, and gives privacy to the interior spaces.

Margarida House | Aranda, Pigem, and Vilalta

Margarida is a detached house built in Olot and designed to be used as a primary residence. Two aspects characterize its location: the fact that it faces the street, and the slope thereof. Behind the gray wall bordering the site stands a white block, split into two floors that contain most of the rooms in the house. Within this block is a lower one containing the kitchen and, on a lower floor, the garage. The design includes just two more elements: a projection that produces a horizontal line of shade and divides the large opening of the main block into two, and three vertical metal pipes corresponding to the chimney.

The architecture is along simple and rigid lines, using a restricted range of shapes, elements, and materials. The various structural elements are skillfully joined together, and shapes are clean.

The color and materials not only help accentuate the contrasts between the different sections, but also provide an understanding of the building as an architectural dialog. The various finishes allow each element to be identified and differentiated so that the building as a whole is enriched by the nuances and variations between each of its constituent parts.

Architects: Aranda, Pigem, and Vilalta
Location: Olot, Gerona, Spain
Photography: Eugeni Pons

The design includes a horizontal projection, which divides the opening of the main block, and three vertical metal pipes corresponding to the chimney.

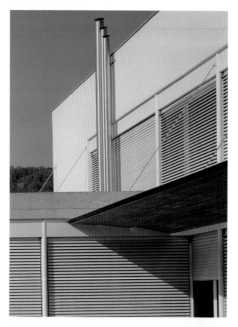

The use of different finishes distinguishes
the individual elements.

House in Dornach | Morger & Degelo

South of Basel lies the town of Dornach, where this light, compact construction stands in an elevated position near a crossroad.

The layout and height of the building were dictated by the view to the south and by the desire for privacy from other buildings to the north. Therefore, while the north entrance allows only glimpses of the outside and the side windows have only selective views, the south side is glazed and completely open to the exterior.

This modular cedar-wood construction has an approximate surface area of 2,000 square feet (200 square meters) on two floors. It presents a clear contrast between the lower floor, which is open in plan, and the upper floor, which is divided up by sliding panels.

The south side of the lower floor is completely glazed a series of large windows, with blue frames also made of cedar wood, provide enormous amounts of natural light in this totally open space.

The load of the house is borne by the side walls and window frames, providing great freedom in the internal layout.

Architects: Morger & Degelo
Location: Dornach, Switzerland
Photography: Ruedi Walti

Although the building is structurally consistent with the typical
wooden buildings
of the area, the
trapezoidal shape
of the design gives
it a dynamism all its own.

The south side of the building is completely
glazed on the
ground floor, and
has large windows
on the upper floor.

Thanks to the way in which the windows have been placed, there are marvelous views from the south side of the house.

Glass House in Almelo | Dirk Jan Postel

This house is an unadorned container, with dimensions based on the repetition of a module the size of a simple bedroom. The front and sides of the building are completely covered in screen-printed glass in the form of an external ventilated sheet, ignoring the presence of windows and forming a taut skin interrupted only by the entrance porch and garage door. This smooth surface acts like a huge screen, reflecting the outside world all day but providing glimpses of life inside the house at night.

The box structure looks closed and cold from the street, but at the rear it is open to the garden through an exquisitely simple glazed extension. Here, large windows create a direct connection between inside and outside. The rest of this rear wall is covered in horizontal wooden panels, also arranged as a ventilated facade. Internal walls have birch-wood cladding, to provide a warm and welcoming atmosphere.

The construction is refined and the design rigorous. The house is the result of a minimalist plan, which complies with very few formal requirements, and has the detached role of architectural structures that are metaphorically removed from their surroundings.

Architect: Dirk Jan Postel
Location: Almelo, Netherlands
Photography: Jordi Miralles

With views over the garden, the rear facade is more permeable and warm. The area of glass that projects from the building is an internal terrace, an intermediate space connecting the house to the exterior.

House in Staufen | Morger & Degelo

This house is part of a residential complex built to satisfy a demand for housing in the area between Geneva and St. Gallen in Switzerland. In spite of the ecological, landscape-related and emotional consequences, the crops previously grown on the land were replaced by houses situated near the country's main communication arteries.

The garden, which is the only vestige of the past, plays a leading role in this compact design. At first sight the living areas look like one big room, visible from all the various parts of the house. This room is surrounded by the patio, the porch, and the facilities, and is open to the exterior. The continuous wooden floor and white walls accentuate the fluidity of this living area.

By contrast, the service areas have been designed as compact rooms, with different finishes applied to reflect their various functions. While all external walls are of bare concrete, the interior finishes range from plywood paneling in the entrance hall, glass tiling in the bathroom, textiles lining the walls of the dressing room, and black paint, reminiscent of the soot on ancient chimneys, in the kitchen.

Architects: Morger & Degelo
Location: Staufen, Switzerland
Photography: Ruedi Walti

House in Germany | David Chipperfield Architects

To reach this house, in a residential area, you have to walk up from the lowest part of the plot via a brick stairway. From here you can walk diagonally across the site to reach the back garden, leaving the side of the building and its main entrance behind you.

The house is on three floors, with the lower floor absorbing the slope in the land and the two upper floors arranged around a patio facing the rear garden. The staircase is a fundamental structure because it links the various areas of each level to one another. The lowest floor is split into two areas, while on the second and third floors the position of the vertical nucleus reduces the surface area, thereby achieving optimum connection between the spaces.

A feeling of intimacy pervades the entire house. Rooms have good links with the exterior, while being visually separate.

The side overlooking the street has almost no windows on the upper floors. This gives the building an introspective appearance, isolating it from the world outside so that it focuses instead on the interior landscape of patio and back garden.

The texture of the walls has been achieved using handcrafted bricks, which are combined with other surfaces of glass and steel.

Architects: David Chipperfield Architects
Location: Germany
Photography: Stefan Müller

Ground floor   Upper floor

A major contrast in textures
exists between the ruggedness
of the brickwork and the
smooth, shiny surfaces of
the glazing. The house is a
simple and harmonious
geometrical composition.
The openings in the building
have been carefully considered,
so that the concept of fullness,
rather than emptiness, always
predominates. This characteristic,
together with the simplicity of
the facades, conveys a feeling of stillness and permanence.

Homes in Amsterdam | Claus en Kaan Architekten

Felix Claus and Kees Kaan have carried out small projects in the district of Haarlemmerbuurt, to restore monuments and construct new buildings. The architects themselves define their work in medical terms, as microsurgery operations.

On Binnenwieringerstraat, work was carried out on a very small existing structure, which was just 11.5 feet (3.5 meters) wide and 26 feet (8 meters) deep. The architects therefore decided to use an adjacent space to house all the facilities and installations required, so that the original building could be used to create a comfortable apartment. In fact, as a result of the renovation, the old structure now contains only three rooms. The work has thus allowed the original structure to be preserved, with the traditional construction details intact (which would be impossible to reproduce today), and without having to damage them to install facilities, staircases, ventilation ducts, and so on.

However, on Haarlemmerstraat, the architects decided to demonstrate the specific and contemporary nature of their work. In fact, the project is a compendium of facades from many different eras,

Architects: Claus en Kaan Architekten
Location: Amsterdam, Netherlands
Photography: Ger van de Vlugt

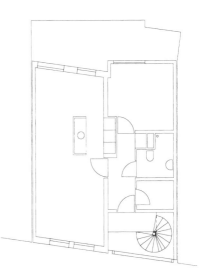

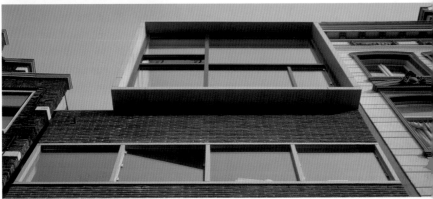

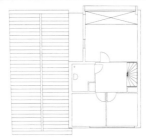

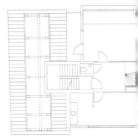

Since the exit from the hotel next door had to be
retained, the
architects decided
to make the most of
it and turn it into
a shared access for
the two buildings.
Not only has the
residual space
been made use of,
but it has also
acquired new meaning
as a semi-public space.

Residential and Office Buildings | Léon & Wohlhage

These buildings are in Hamburg-Hammerbrook, a southern district of Hamburg with many industrial buildings and offices.

Both buildings stand on a triangular site. The position of the two main blocks leaves a clear semi-public space in the middle, connected to the street, and creating an access area to the VTG office building. This building has a smooth surface on the side facing the street, which projects an image of tranquillity, while behind it four triangular blocks with a more striking appearance face the center of the site.

The shape of the exterior is also reflected inside: the corridors of the double rows of offices open onto triangular empty spaces. These constitute a vertical connection between all the floors, as well as making the corridors wider.

The housing block is independent of the offices, and consists of two-bedroom apartments lit from a gallery, as well as apartments overlooking the garden. Access to the apartments is from four staircases, with wide entrance lobbies two stories high.

Architect: Léon & Wohlhage
Location: Hamburg, Germany
Photography: Klaus Frahm

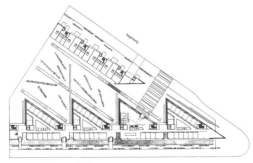

General plan

A free composition of large green concrete panels marks each end of the VTG building. The double-glazed facade overlooking the street protects the building from traffic noise, and allows the offices to be ventilated naturally.

452

Sirch Manufacturing Plant | Baumschlager & Eberle

The task of expanding a medium-sized industrial complex in a contemporary way is one that Baumschlager & Eberle tackled in 1995, with the new showroom building for the Altenried timber processing plant in the Bavarian community of Hergatz. The wooden building, clad in Siberian larch, is perfectly in tune with its surroundings, its arched facades drawing an analogy between the building and the rolling landscape.

In this case, the building presented a similar challenge. Also located in the southern highlands of Germany, it stands on a gently sloping hill and consists of a stretched cube. Because it blends with the landscape and other residential buildings, it does not stand out when viewed from the access road. Only from the east is there a complete view of the building, when you can see both of the two floors.

The two levels of this wooden structure are contiguous, but tension is created between them by the use of different materials on each of their facades. The lower floor, set into the ground and strengthened on three sides by solid concrete retaining walls, is covered in translucent panels, whereas the long side of the upper level is covered in strips of larch wood.

Architects: Baumschlager & Eberle

Location: Böhen, Germany

Photography: Eduard Hueber

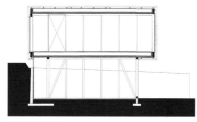

Cross section

Because the lower level is slightly elevated, it appears to hover above its supporting structure. Large windows all along both front facades provide natural light on the main level.

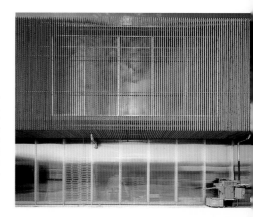

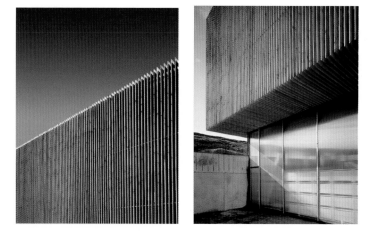

Optimal Printing Facilities | Carsten Roth

This industrial building, situated southwest of Schwerin in Germany, is a CD factory, which operates 24 hours a day. The venture had grown very quickly but pragmatically, and needed to expand its complex as quickly as possible, on a limited budget, and without interrupting production. The new building, linked to the CD production floor by conveyor belts, is both functionally and structurally complex, which is expressed in the facade.

The entrance is a vast area, which welcomes the 250 employees working on each of the four daily shifts, as well as accommodating the emergency staircases in a single unit hidden behind automatic doors. The atmosphere is very similar to the foyer of a theater or museum. The longitudinal, oblique, and vertical openings on the facade provide wide views of the landscape from all areas.

Like works of art in a glass case, the main supporting pillars which run from the floor to the roof dominate the interior, including the cafeteria kitchen, providing flexibility on the lower floor.

Architect: Carsten Roth
Location: Schwerin, Germany
Photography: Klaus Frahm/Artur

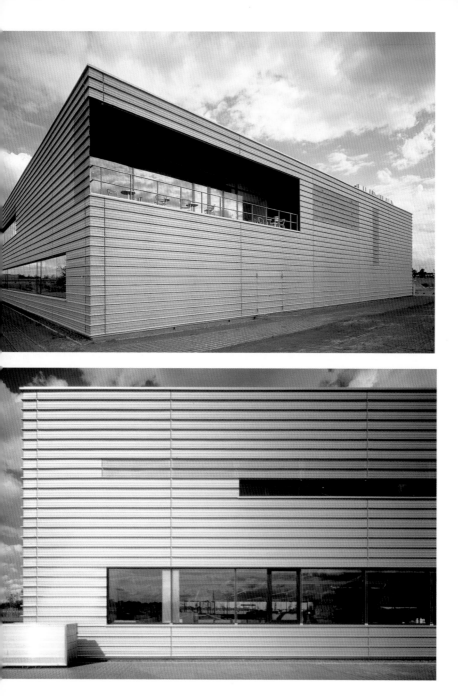

Graf Offices | Baumschlager & Eberle

The original building of the Graf electricity company had to be enlarged, by adding two additional modules, to form a compact corporate complex. The clients wanted the whole building to have great visual impact. The new structures had to be recognized immediately, but the complex as a whole also had to demonstrate perfect unity.

The conditions were difficult and delicate. The existing office building was not noted for its attractiveness, and, furthermore, the geological conditions were not favorable. Groundwater levels were very high, and there were innumerable layers of gravel, some of which were up to 1,000 feet (300 meters) deep. This made designing the structural foundations extremely difficult.

To assist movement and communication, the additional production and storage premises were placed in a square module at ground-floor level, as a link to the original building. This module was then connected to the existing one by a bridge, a symbolic building that joins the two areas and houses the company's administrative offices.

The walls of the previous construction were masked by timber cladding. The new building, conceived as a gigantic glass and concrete beam, sits over powerful lights shining from below.

Architects: Baumschlager & Eberle
Location: Dornbirn, Austria
Photography: Eduard Hueber

The orange color of the building makes it stand out so that its offices
can be clearly seen from
afar as if to advertise
the electricity
company. The nature
of the beam allowed
a large number of
windows to be
installed, which
are as high and
wide as possible.

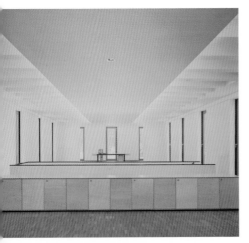

Inside the beam the
reinforced concrete
structure was left
unclad and painted
white, to emphasize the functionality of the building.

Mercator, Phase One | Paul de Ruiter

This building is the first phase of a complex dedicated to science. The client gave great importance to technological development and wanted to stress environmental factors. A further condition was that the first phase of the project should have great architectural presence, which would be the basis for the development of subsequent phases of the complex.

The intention was to design a facade that would be economically efficient and project the image required by the client. The result is a combination of external glass with insulating properties, extending from the ground floor to the roof, and fine sheets of translucent, metalized mesh that form a sunscreen. The air trapped between the two surfaces is extracted by a mechanical ventilation system. The facade therefore acts as a protective envelope, insulating the interior from extreme outside temperatures. The mesh does not obstruct the view from within, and can be rolled up, using an electric system, into bands 6 feet (1.8 metres) wide, allowing individuals to control light levels.

The internal pillar structure allows the facade to be continuous, interrupted only by two openings at the sides. The shape of the building is extremely simple: a rectangular body resting on a timber-clad platform.

Architect: Paul de Ruiter

Location: Nijmegen, Netherlands

Photography: Rien van Rijthoven

As the day progresses and the angle of the sun's rays changes, the facade
reflects the light
differently, so
that the appearance
of this vast surface
alters many times.

Office Buildings in Zurich | Romero & Schaefle

A firm of engineers purchased two mixed residential and commercial buildings in the center of Zurich, near the railway station. The task they assigned was to renovate the buildings to accommodate a company with 80 employees. Demolishing the buildings was out of the question, for town planning reasons.

The firm asked for the structure to be lighter and more open, while retaining the load-bearing walls of the building. To achieve this, the staircase was replaced by a vertical transparent unit with a glass lift and a new staircase made of steel. At the ground-floor entrance level, large windows were installed into the whole facade overlooking the rear courtyard, to bring the exterior landscape into this open and luminous environment.

A small building in the rear courtyard, now housing a cafeteria with a roof terrace, was modified and linked to the entrance floor by a streamlined, see-through passageway.

The rear facade was completely renovated. Large fixed windows run from floor to ceiling on each level.

Introducing the same idea of transparency that was applied to the rear facade, the front of the building overlooking the street was also renovated, but only at ground level.

Architects: Romero & Schaefle
Location: Zurich, Switzerland
Photography: Heinrich Helfenstein,
   Alexander Troehler

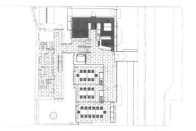

Ground floor

Book Technology Center in Marne-la-Vallée | Dominique Perrault

This center in Marne-la-Vallée is in the district of Bussy-Saint-Georges, near the A-4 freeway and the RER A railroad linking the town of Marne-la-Vallée to the center of Paris.

The site is completely flat, with hardly any other nearby buildings or references to the surrounding countryside, or to the building itself. The hermetically sealed buildings could therefore easily be taken for land art.

The axis of the design is an internal covered roadway used for distribution and communication between the various areas of the center. Workshops and warehouses line this road, and access to the site is from a single entry point on the north side.

The facades are covered in a layer of aluminum, consisting of opaque panels. Most of these are fixed, and the ones that are movable are driven by electric mechanisms. The whole design is extremely uncluttered and clean, its beauty arising from the obvious absence of all superfluous detail.

Architect: Dominique Perrault
Location: Bussy-Saint-Georges, France
Photography: Georges Fessy

The basic function of the technology center is to store
and preserve rare
collections or works
of reference, in order
to make space available
in the storerooms and
archives of libraries in
higher education establishments.

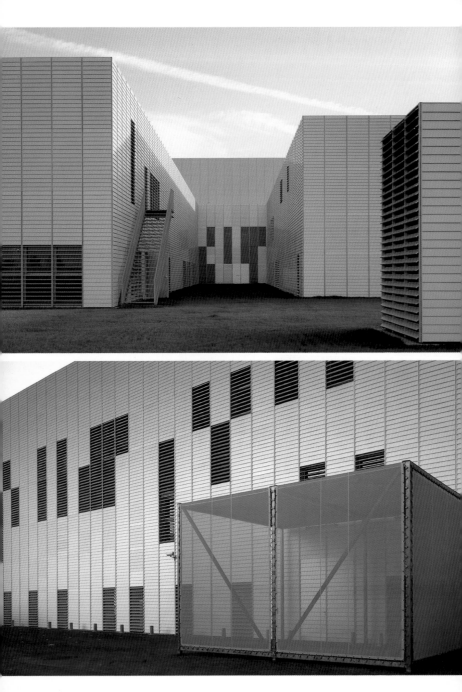

Lagertechnik Wolfurt Office Building and Garage | Baumschlager & Eberle

This site is surrounded by very different features: dense housing to the south, a highway to the north, a freeway overpass to the east, and cultivated fields to the west.

This building has a clear, emphatic, and conceptual shape. Essentially it consists of two rectangular blocks made of various materials: bare concrete, unpainted wooden shutters, panels, and translucent glass.

The two contrasting blocks face the street. One is tall and thin, and contains the multistory parking garage. It has a continuous, translucent facade through which you can just make out the blurred outlines of the automobiles. Beside it is a concrete framework, with full and empty spaces created by an arrangement of sliding timber panels. The regularity of this facade's concrete structure gives it a uniform rhythm.

The relationship between outside and inside is interesting, in the way in which the building reflects one type of relationship or the other. Both the position of the building and access to it reflect this relationship, with each part of the design reacting fully to and independently of its neighbor.

Architects: Baumschlager & Eberle
Location: Wolfurt, Austria
Photography: Eduard Hueber

The parking garage, with its translucent facade, overlooks the busy freeway and acts as a barrier between the traffic and the offices in the other building. Panels covering the southwest side of the office building provide protection from solar radiation, while the northeast face consists of bare concrete panels with small horizontal windows flush with the wall.

Foreign Ministry Restaurant | Bernard Desmoulin

A number of offices belonging to the French Foreign Ministry, which had been scattered all over Paris, were recently brought under one roof at no. 244 Boulevard Saint-Germain.

The project is as discreet as it is assertive, and is designed, according to the architect himself, as a passive building that blends with its environment in order to enhance and pay homage to it. The design makes the most of the opportunities afforded by the privileged environment, creating the conditions in which small and often concealed patios can become almost magical places where nature, the passage of time, and the seasons become a reality in the middle of the city.

Only a partially buried construction could satisfy all the requirements of the project, and at the same time restore the garden. The glazed facade of the ground floor continues along the ground in the garden, where it becomes a skylight through which daylight floods into the underground restaurant.

Desmoulin defines the design as "a glass square that is a well of reflections, a mirror reproducing the front of the building on the ground, and vice versa, and a trap to ensnare the greenery of the hidden gardens and the architecture of the seventh *arrondissement.*"

Architect: Bernard Desmoulin
Location: Paris, France
Photography: Hervé Abbadie

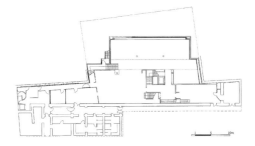

Upper floor

Ground floor

This space once housed two prefabricated single-story units, which were used as an office restaurant. Bernard Desmoulin's design removed the need for these units.

Río Florida Restaurant | Ercilla & Campo

Hardly any modern design tradition exists for lodges and summerhouses set in large parks or public areas.

The suitability of these buildings for their surroundings lies in the concept of quick, easy assembly and, therefore, the use of light materials with the right technology.

The difficulties presented by the site suggested the idea of splitting the building into three interconnected pavilions, each with a separate function. One is a restaurant, one a bar, and one a terrace.

Construction is defined by the structure. A simple, three-dimensional framework marks out and unites the pavilions. The building as a whole is conceived as a set of pieces prepared in a workshop and later assembled on site. The collapsible structure, made from Oregon pine, is held together with pieces of galvanized steel.

In the first version of the project the idea was to use three different casings: wood for the bar unit, glass for the restaurant, and the bare framework itself for the terrace. In the end, the wood of the bar was also replaced by glass, since the aim throughout was to give a feeling of dining out in the middle of the woods. Architecture is kept to a minimum to give way to nature.

Architects: Ercilla & Campo
Location: Vitoria, Spain
Photography: César San Millán

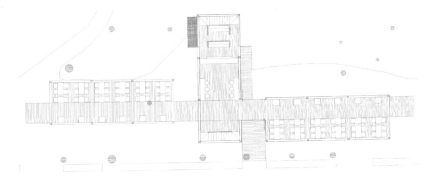

Ground plan

Floors, trimmings, and furniture
are all made from the same material.
Both of the enclosed, transparent blocks are encased in glass.

Educational Workshops | Marc Barani

Near the castle of Mouans-Sartoux between Cannes and Grasse, these educational workshops for children and teenagers consist of three different units: the workshops themselves, a lecture hall (and music room), and an open-air sculpture park surrounded by trees and sky.

The building is composed of harmonious rectangles whose balance lends peace to the open spaces. There is a clear correspondence between the blocks and the movement of people around them.

The architect comments: "The building is laid out on a hill and marked out by two routes. The first leads toward the center and more intimate spaces flooded with light. The second route opens outward to the workshops, the castle, and the woods. Its architecture is thus intricately connected to the surroundings and forms a part of the educational program."

The visitor's imagination is teased into the desire to discover more. This project does not reveal itself at first sight, and so counters the culture of the direct and immediate. By working with contrasts and discrepancies in scale, it aims to inspire thoughtfulness. For example, the solidity of the rear facade, on the way into the complex, contrasts with the large glass surfaces of the main entrance, which are discovered later on.

Architect: Marc Barani

Location: Mouans-Sartoux, France

Photography: S. Demailly

The three facades
differ in response
to their surroundings.
The blind northeast
face is like an
extension of the base
of the castle, while
to the northwest the
openings in the wall
facing the woods are
an ambiguous prelude
to the grand glass
facade of the entrance.
On the southeast side,
visitors cross a space
that runs between one
of the old walls of the fort and the workshops.

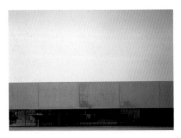

Ecological Secondary School | Baumschlager & Eberle

For the last couple of years Mädar, once a poor village near the border with Switzerland, has been trying to gain recognition as an ecological community. The town plan includes a series of public squares linked by paths. This pedestrian-friendly network becomes denser toward the new center, where all the cultural attractions are to be found (including the Community Center, also designed by Baumschlager & Eberle in 1995).

The new Ecological Secondary School building has greatly improved the town center. The position of the two blocks, which are separated at ground level, not only creates two new open spaces (a public square and the school playground), but also sets clear boundaries.

Both blocks – the four-story school building and the gym, a third of which is buried underground – are compact, thus minimizing energy consumption. The structure is a mixture of wood and glass enveloped in turn by a glass casing that acts as a ventilation system. Depending on the position of the sun, shifting transparencies change the building's appearance: sometimes it appears to vanish in low light, and sometimes it mirrors its surroundings.

Architects: Baumschlager & Eberle
Location: Mäder, Vorarlberg, Austria
Photography: Eduard Hueber

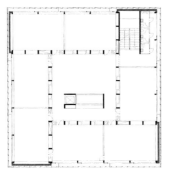

Floor plan

The glass walls, a central skylight, and the windows in the wooden interior walls provide natural light for the whole building, despite the large area of the lower floor. At each level, seven classrooms are arranged around a central recreation area. The building combines ecology, economy, and quality of space.

Rural Dwelling in France | Gouwy/Grima/Rames

Perched on an arid hilltop, this house is half underground, spreading out beneath a large terrace with views over the plateau of Gramat.

The decision to bury the north side of the house was made in order to insulate it from the nearby freeway and shelter it from north winds, as well as by a desire to integrate a decidedly modern design into a landscape dominated by stone walls. The owner, a retired contractor, was not afraid to build a "roofless" home.

The house is set behind a stone wall, which extends 138 feet (42 meters) to the south. You approach the house along a path that winds through juniper bushes until you finally reach the western end of the facade. Another low wall, perpendicular to the front one, encloses the yard and shows the way into the house. From here a corridor leads to the rooms and also continues north across the yard.

The rooms open out onto a rectangular lawn bounded by the swimming pool and low walls covered in vine leaves, providing an oasis in the middle of this arid land.

Architects: Gouwy/Grima/Rames
Location: Seniergues, France
Photography: Patrick Tourneboeuf

The use of limestone is reminiscent of the traditional buildings of the region.

The stone was quarried from the many sunken walls in the area.

The use of limestone allows the house to blend into the
landscape very successfully.

Large windows
light the
living room and bedrooms.

Graz Technical University | Riegler Riewe

These Austrian architects base most of their projects on the rectangular grid, with its inherent potential for order and growth through which rhythm and drama can unfold. Their most radical use of this basic strategy can be seen in the design of the Technical University building in Graz.

A group of eight buildings was made up of enclosed blocks clearly separated from their surroundings and laid out in a rectangular grid. These buildings, each three floors high, form a small-scale urban patchwork, connected by passages, streets, and squares planted with various types of trees.

Each building consists of two blocks separated by a gap. The offices face south, the classrooms and libraries north. The blocks are linked by bridges so that the various institutes and faculties are connected according to the level or block in which they are located. At street level, the space has been left empty to allow for the free flow of pedestrians, despite the severity of the grid.

There are also enough open spaces offering light and fresh air to refresh the senses and stimulate the intellect.

Architects: Riegler Riewe
Location: Graz, Styra, Austria
Photography: Paul Ott

The eight buildings are each divided into two blocks and
connected by passages,
streets, and squares
where different kinds of
trees have been planted.

Site plan

527

Rural School in Paspels | Valerio Olgiati

Olgiati's concept for this rural school in Paspels is based on keeping signs and materials to an absolute minimum. The building is a concrete parallelepiped with no decoration on its four outside walls, other than that provided by the openings necessary for classroom windows and the front door. Different window frames have been used to mark the different areas within, giving the exterior some indication of the hierarchy of these areas. The frames of the classroom windows are mounted inside the wall, producing pronounced shadows when seen from the outside. In areas not used for classes, such as the corridors, the frames are mounted on the outside, flush to the wall. These trimmings are made of an aluminum alloy with the appearance of rusted bronze.

In this irregularly shaped block, the rooms have been placed in the corners, leaving the central area as additional empty space. Every classroom has one continuous window and each of the four wings of the extra space also end in a window. The near-rectangular geometry of the ground floor seems to have been dislocated by some seismic shift. In fact, the outer perimeter of the building is not completely straight. Only the inner walls are at right angles.

Architect: Valerio Olgiati

Location: Paspels, Switzerland

Photography: Valerio Olgiati, Heinrich Helfenstein

Concrete has been
used for the
interior walls,
except in the
classrooms, where
walls, floors,
and ceilings are lined in wood.

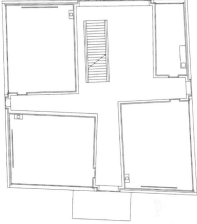

Top floor

Faculty of Media Sciences | Varis Architects

The brief received by Varis Architects for this project required that, when in use, the classrooms could either be in total darkness (to allow the use of projectors) or lit by natural daylight (for more theoretical classes).

The facade of the main block is completely covered in long horizontal bands of aluminum. Some of these act as shutters, which can be adjusted mechanically up to 85 degrees. Thus the building itself opens and closes to let in or shut out the light.

The narrow, glass facade of one tip of the building cuts into the urban landscape, on a street from which you can also enter the lobby of the faculty. From here, you can reach other floors via stairs and lifts.

The basement houses technical workshops where images and sounds are created and manipulated: set, control room, make-up, IT rooms, radio studios, darkrooms, and video-editing suites.

The classrooms are on the upper floors of the main building. The faculty's management and administration offices are in the wing that juts out toward the city.

Architects: Varis Architects
Location: Barcelona, Spain
Photography: David Cardelús, Mihail Moldoveanu

The Faculty of
Media Sciences is
located in the
historic quarter
of the city of
Barcelona.
Surrounded by
high-density housing,
the building is part
of an arts and
educational complex that enriches the life of the area.

The bar-restaurant is on the ground floor, with wide windows looking onto the square. This is the chief meeting place and social center of the building. It is two floors high, full of light, and simply furnished, mainly in beechwood. A loft above the bar houses the library.

The Dojo | Patrick Berger

Among the variety of different buildings on the outskirts of Brétigny-sur-Orge, the Dojo (judo hall) marks one of the boundaries of the city. Covering the front of the building are two huge flat planes of wood, 215 feet (66 meters) long and 10 feet (3 meters) from the ground. Their surfaces incline slightly outward to protect the platform at the entrance. A large, continuous skylight illuminates the interior with natural light, while light also washes over the broken planes of the wooden facade.

The laminated wooden structure holding up the roof is supported on big, round, concrete pillars next to the outer walls, which add to the sense of weight.

The sports facility has two functions, training and competition. These activities take place on different levels, separated by a flight of stairs. The changing rooms are under these. Another flight of stairs runs lengthwise up from the entrance hall.

This is architecture to excite the senses, with its great, solid mass containing a block of shadow, the weight of the roof pressing down on concrete pillars, the texture of its sheets of wood, and its expanse of paving.

Architect: Patrick Berger

Location: Brétigny-sur-Orge, France

Photography: J.M. Monthiers, J.Y. Cousseau

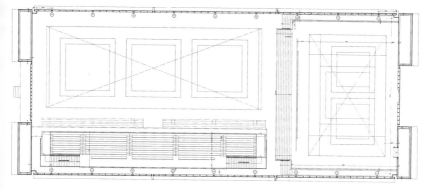

Top floor

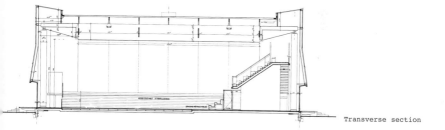

Transverse section

From the gravel surface outside and the paved wooden platform at the entrance,
to the interior
especially designed
for judo, this is
architecture that
excites the senses.

Building on the Aveiro Campus | Eduardo Souto de Moura

The urban layout of the campus and the terms of the brief from the university set some clear guidelines for this building, the Aveiro Department of Geosciences. These were: the total area to be built on, the maximum height, length, and width of the building, the percentage of the area to be designated for traffic, and the material (red brick) to be used on the facades. With the ground rules established, the building – a box divided by a central corridor – took shape almost without further discussion. It would be inappropriate to judge Souto de Moura's work by the way the building is laid out on the site or on its size, since these were determined in advance.

While the building is thus not minimalist in shape, it is in the choice of materials, the finishing touches, the control of light, and the atmosphere of the interior space. It is an austere building, conveying a total rejection of any unnecessary architectural frills. It shows enormous attention to detail, with the aim of minimizing the impact of these details in the final result. The intention was to leave the structure undisguised in order to reveal the principles of its construction, and to try to make abstract geometrical sense of the sum of its parts

Architect: Eduardo Souto de Moura

Location: Aveiro, Portugal

Photography: Christian Richters

One of the most characteristic details of Souto de Moura's work is perhaps his habit of presenting noble materials in unusual ways. In this case, for example, slabs of pink marble are rimmed with metal.

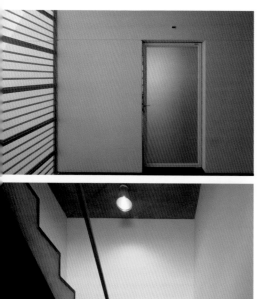

In this building
the rooms are
unadorned and
furniture kept to the bare essentials.

Faculty of Journalism | Karljosef Schattner

This piece of work is set among the historic buildings of the Catholic University of Eichstätt where an architect has to consider the surroundings in planning any new building or extension.

It was decided that the block should not be subdivided, and should be on a grand scale. Like the building next to it, the Faculty of Journalism is split into two parts, of similar size but not matching in plan, joined by a glass lobby containing a corridor, stairs, and connecting bridge. Another block, which follows the slight slope of the street, houses the television and video studios. The main facade, which looks onto the street, has six rows of windows. The roof is a simple structure of steel beams, with the air-conditioning unit positioned underneath it.

There are few openings into the building, so that the simple lines of the structure acquire great importance, standing out like graphics. The entrance is to the rear, where the surface is flat. In contrast to the baroque facades of its neighbors, this building has only one, great doorway, which has a subtle join across the lintel.

Architect: Karljosef Schattner

Location: Eichstätt, Germany

Photography: Atelier Klaus Kinold

As well as the spacious lobby and the elevator tower, the building also houses the radio studios, the workshop, and a courtyard.

General plan

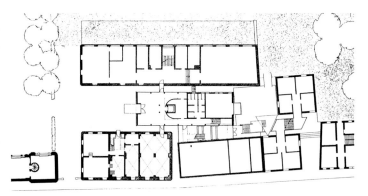

University Museum in Alicante | Alfredo Payá

At one end of the campus, and bounded by the freeway with mountains in the distance, the striking image of a round box floating in a vast hollowed-out space is our first sight of this building. It looks inaccessible. At the foot of the concavity the ground dips toward the entrance, and the visitor, like a mole, discovers a deeply excavated route through the various rooms.

The stones surrounding the building seem always to have been there, as if they were dug up during the excavations. The ground becomes a venue for a variety of artistic activities.

The courtyard is an empty space linking the different parts of the museum, as well as providing a place for reflection and repose. From here you can reach all sections of the building, including the galleries of the general museum, the open-air auditorium, the indoor hall, and, of course, the box itself.

These four sections are all on one floor, laid out two by two. On one side there are the museum galleries, linked by areas that visitors walk through, and on the other the auditoriums, which face each other and can be joined together. The front of the stage of the covered hall can be folded away, so that this room can also be incorporated into another one.

Architect: Alfredo Payá
Location: Alicante, Spain
Photography: Miguel Ángel Valero

The box is the main
feature of the complex,
and houses the permanent
collection. It is very
tall, and floats as
if weightless. A small horizontal opening leads to the courtyard.

The proportions of the
box and the way light
is used give it a sense
of stretching to infinity.
The double-skinned walls
conceal the building's
installations and audiovisual
equipment, such as projectors, screens, and videos.

Longitudinal section

Krems Art Gallery | Adolf Krischanitz

The design for this project deals with the dialog between an old building, which used to be a tobacco factory, and a new block under construction. Together they will house exhibition spaces. An inner courtyard linking these two parallel parts is roofed in glass so that it can also be used for exhibitions or functions.

Together, the old and the new building create a series of areas adapted and structured in different ways. As well as the exhibition spaces, they also contain a reading room, a lobby, a café, offices, storage rooms, and rooms for technical equipment.

The original industrial character of the old building has been kept by conserving architectural features of historical significance, such as pillars and windows. In the design for the new spaces, materials have been used with restraint so that works of art can be displayed to maximum effect.

Architect: Adolf Krischanitz
Location: Krems, Austria
Photography: Margherita Spiluttini

The character of the building dominates
the interior. Windows, beams, and
pillars all add to the effect.

Austrian Stand at the Frankfurt Book Fair | Adolf Krischanitz

Among all the sites designated for stands at the Frankfurt Book Fair, the Austrian stand is located just where it should be, in the center of the surrounding space. The country was to be represented at the fair for three days, with a stand in the middle of a big rectangular public square, bordered by other buildings.

The shape and position of the stand were partly determined by O.M. Ungers' landscape design for this square, at the center of which an obelisk rises from a circular fountain. The inner wall of Krischanitz's creation faces toward this central space, to which there is no access, while the outer wall forms a continuous glass screen facing the rest of the square.

Painted in white, the building is almost invisible: the most eye-catching features are the lights between the beams and the literary quotes by Robert Musil on the outer screen. The legibility of this text depends on the time of day; the larger letters, in white, face outward while the smaller ones, in black, are meant to be read from the inside.

Four tangential outer ramps provide access and create a centrifugal movement through the exhibition space.

Architect: Adolf Krischanitz

Location: Frankfurt, Germany

Photography: Margherita Spiluttini

There are two kinds of text on the glass screen. The larger white text is intended to be read from outside, from a distance. Its color contrasts with the dark interior of the stand during the day. Once inside, the text is read from closer up and is therefore smaller, in black to stand out against the daylight coming in from outside.

MA Gallery | Hiroyuki Arima + Urban Fourth

The MA Gallery is situated in the Genkai national park, a hilly region between the mountains and the sea, two hours from the city of Fukuoka. The project includes an exhibition space and a studio for the client, an artist. It is made up of five blocks set on top of a steep slope 55 feet (17 meters) high.

Various different materials have been used in its construction: cement, cedar wood, corrugated polycarbonate, steel plates, and wire mesh. The spaces are flexible and flow into each other. An abundant supply of natural light was required to illuminate the exhibition rooms, which are also used for concerts, and the artist's studio, which was designed to be set apart from the rest of the building for greater privacy.

The rocky surface of the slope meant that each floor and block needed to be built with its own self-supporting structure. In this way the surroundings were not greatly altered and the pillars could be placed discreetly on the different levels, without following too rigid a pattern.

Architects: Hiroyuki Arima + Urban Fourth

Location: Itoshima-gun, Fukuoka, Japan

Photography: Koji Okamoto

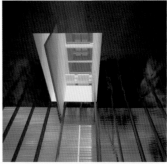

The upper floor of the gallery is used for exhibitions and as a viewpoint,
looking out over the
plain to Lake Genka-nada.
A glass display case
not only holds works
of art, but also reflects
light down to the lower
floors, emphasizing the
flow of the space between
the different levels.

River & Rowing Museum | David Chipperfield

This museum on the River Thames houses displays of rowing boats, historical archives about the sport and the river itself, and a large collection illustrating the history of the local town of Henley. Its outward appearance is based on the traditional wooden barns of Oxfordshire and the boathouses of Henley.

The building consists of two parts: a spacious, transparent ground floor for public events, and the galleries, protected from the weather, on the upper floor.

A look at the choice of materials and arrangement of details makes it easy to understand the way the museum works. This is most clearly shown in the inverted construction of the closed boxes that float over the glass floor of the entrance level. The two boat rooms on the first floor are paneled in oak and lit only by round skylights, creating contained exhibition spaces that encourage concentration. This effect contrasts with the open, glassed-in spaces of the entrance level. The interpretation of the project thus complements the architectural composition.

The museum is right next to the river, and set on a raised wooden platform extending out from the building.

Architect: David Chipperfield
Location: London, United Kingdom
Photography: Richard Bryant

Traditional sloping roofs were used in a more
abstract version of the
local architecture.
The idea was to balance
convention and invention,
the figurative and
the abstract.

Carl Liner Museum | Gigon & Guyer

This museum in Appenzell, Switzerland, is dedicated to the work of artists Carl August Liner and his son Carl Walter.

The rooms were not designed especially for the work of these artists, but are well-suited to the display of some of their paintings and for exhibitions of modern art. These are simple spaces, which do not attempt to compete with the art they contain. They have a minimum of detail, concrete floors and natural lighting through skylights in the sloping roofs.

The rooms are relatively small, creating a focused atmosphere in which each painting can receive proper attention. The exhibition space is divided into ten rooms, diminishing in size from south to north.

Two side windows offer views to the outside world and aid orientation within the building. At the northern end there are a small reading room and a room for video showings. The largest space is the lobby where tickets are sold and which is also used as a lecture room.

The sloping roofs echo both the traditional houses of the region and the indented roofs of industrial buildings.

Architects : Gigon & Guyer
Location: Appenzell, Switzerland
Photography: H. Helfenstein

The roofs and outer walls are covered in chromed steel plates, which reflect a very diffuse light with no color distortion. The way the plates overlap and their striking gray color recall traditional local architecture. The use of the same material for walls and roofs creates an irregular shape, like a small mountain against the massive backdrop of the Alps.

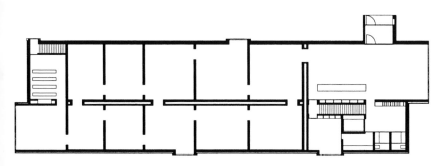

Plan

Natural light filters in
from high up the walls.

Vitra Seminary | Tadao Ando

The main challenges in designing this building in Germany, near the borders of Switzerland and France, were how to fit it into its surroundings and how it was to be entered from the site, which is completely flat. In an attempt to preserve the surrounding woodland and gardens, it was sunk into the ground and its height restricted. Simple geometric shapes, rectangles and circles, were used to create a design in which solid forms contrast with emptiness to produce rich interior spaces. Great care had to be taken in positioning the structure on the site, since it had to fit in alongside Frank O. Gehry's Vitra Museum of Design and an Oldenburg sculpture, which stands between the two buildings.

The building is on two levels. All the rooms open onto a square, sunken courtyard, enclosed by walls on all sides, which reinforces the austere silence of the architecture and expresses a desire to let in the forces of nature – light and wind.

Architect: Tadao Ando

Location: Weil am Rhein, Germany

Photography: Hiroshi Ueda

Site plan

Ando's silent, austere architecture is
in touch with
nature, bringing
light and wind
into the interior.

Freeway Chapel | Guignard & Saner

The idea of building places of worship along the route from Hamburg to Rome was first mooted in Switzerland when the freeway was in the planning stage. Roadside chapels have been successfully established in other parts of the world.

The chapel is situated between the highway and a track along the River Reuss, and reached by a path that gently slopes up from the service area. Two doors lead into a courtyard, which has a fountain in the middle and a bench running around the walls, at the base of the building. From the river track another entrance leads to this spot, and from here the visitor's gaze is drawn to the imposing mountain scenery.

Inside the chapel, beechwood benches are tucked into niches between the concrete pillars. The windows, each made up of two panes of glass 4 inches (10 centimeters) apart, were prefabricated and installed from the outside. The space between the two panes is filled with pieces of broken glass in various shades of green, creating different lighting effects in the interior according to the time of day. At dusk, hanging lamps in the middle of the chapel are lit, reversing the situation.

Architects: Guignard & Saner
Location: Hamburg-Gotthard-Rome Freeway,
Switzerland
Photography: Guignard & Saner, Dominic Büttner

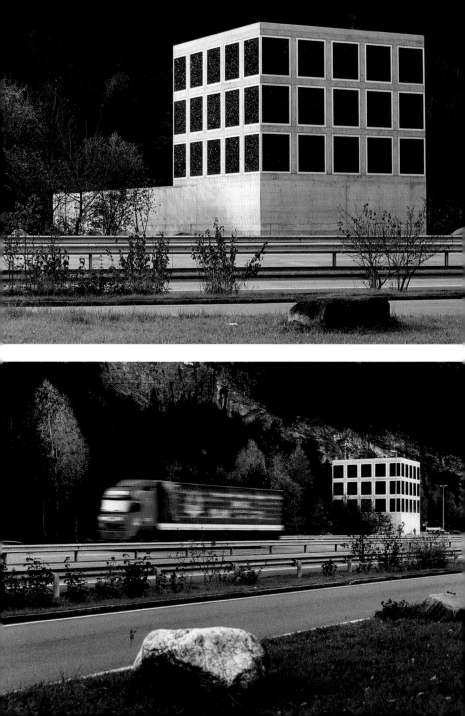

The chapel
is situated
between the
highway and a track along the river.

Plan

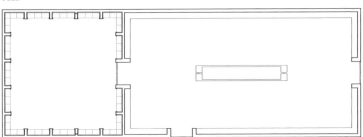

The courtyard is an enclosed and highly controlled space that, nevertheless, frames a vast and distant natural landscape. The interior is an empty cube with no external views. Benches run all around the perimeter.

Crematorium in Berlin | Axel Schultes + Charlotte Frank

The architects here were conscious that their objective was not to try to change the state of mind of those who would use the building, but to provide the right atmosphere in which people could meet, reflect, and collect themselves, a restful place filled with silence. The project grew out of many meditations on religious architecture, spiritual thoughts that helped in an understanding of the abstract requirements of a space for saying farewell to the dead.

References to ancient buildings contributed a great deal to the final result. The idea of a covered central square was adopted, for example, to serve as a meeting place and lead to the rooms arranged around it. Light, which plays an important part throughout the building, is handled with special care in the main hall, where stone columns piercing the roof make holes through which the sun's rays filter. In addition, the edges of the roof do not reach the walls, creating stripes of natural light. Artificial lighting intensifies both these effects.

This is a solemn, monumental building that also succeeds in creating a soothing atmosphere.

Architects: Axel Schultes + Charlotte Frank
Location: Berlin, Germany
Photography: Michael Moran

Three kinds of material were used in this building: bare concrete, glass, and strips of metal for the shutters over most of the windows. Large expanses of concrete and the contrast between solidity and space in the facades, especially to the south, contribute to the impressive effect. The fixed metal blinds filter the light and make the rooms more private.

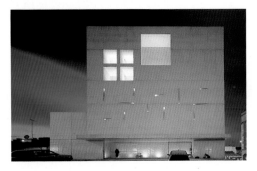

Parish Center in Villalba | Ignacio Vicens, José A. Ramos

This project includes the church, parish hall, and priests' lodgings, on a small plot in a recently developed area near the new station, and next to residential blocks six stories high. The design is austere, to indicate its religious function within the neighborhood.

The style of the facades is abstract and pure, the blank walls creating a monumental effect and only those of the priests' living quarters making any reference to their purpose. The main feature is the church facade, rising above the complex to match the height of the surrounding buildings, and with steps down to the street.

Inside, in contrast to the usual hierarchical arrangement of places of worship, is a square space with no particular focal point, in keeping with the communitarian and collective slant of modern liturgical thinking.

In this building, lighting plays a leading role. A series of parallel concrete screens sift and modulate the light from above, which shines down continuously on the area of worship. In the chancel a single, sloping skylight picks out the area around the font. The same material is used throughout, though with different finishes: bare concrete for the facades, interior walls, and beams of the screens; polished cement for the floors.

Architects: Ignacio Vicens, José A. Ramos
Location: Madrid, Spain
Photography: Eugeni Pons

The main facade of the church features
three types of
window opening:
a square, a square
divided into four,
and a group of
slanting fissures
cut into the wall.
These represent,
respectively, the
Father, the Son,
and the Holy Ghost.
At night they are lit
from inside, like lanterns.

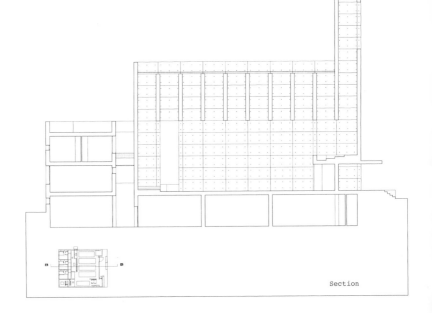

Section

La Animita Chapel | Eduardo Castillo

The design of this chapel grew out of a symbolic interpretation of a popular shape. It is designed around a form that combines spiritual and popular significance, a prism that offers the possibility of a link to the divine.

This is an archetypal shape, a single prism with no seams between walls and roof, which makes the tiny chapel into a unique and ambiguous place, abandoned as it is on the edge of the countryside in a far corner of Chile.

The wood is left exposed to the elements, unvarnished, and with the passing of time is turning a warm gray color, matching the shade of nearby huts.

"What kind of architecture can I hope to build with limited resources, while still believing in its potential? I'm looking for its essence through using strong, ideal, archetypal shapes, full of possibilities, and charged with symbolism that awakens memories, and that is evocative as well as convincing. I look for an easy elegance of form by using closed, conclusive, positive and uncompromising prisms to achieve a simple style. This style is based on a reinterpretation of the rules of popular architecture and founded in an austere reality." (E. Castillo)

Architect: Eduardo Castillo

Location: El Álamo, Concepción, Chile

Photography: Jessica Ramírez Hidalgo

The chapel is the only thing here, a solitary shape apparently abandoned in the middle of nowhere, a strange, ambiguous object. It marks a spot, but will leave no trace when it is gone. It exists without aspiring to permanence.

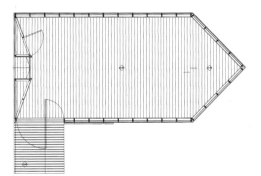

Plan

An *animita* is shrine commemorati a tragic event at particular spo It is usually shape like a little house containing the so of someone who h lost his or her life on the roa

Baño Pavilion | Aranda, Pigem, and Vilalta

Pavilions are isolated, temporary structures, open to onlookers and people passing by.

The brief for this project gave Aranda, Pigem, and Vilalta a certain amount of freedom in designing a central landmark for a park in the province of Gerona. The architects' understanding of landscape is that it combines the natural with the built environment. So they conceived this small building as a sculpture, a work of art for an exceptional setting.

The building is situated at the top of a gently sloping rise. It rests lightly on the ground, as if floating above it. The slight gap between the platform of the pavilion and the mountainside allows rainwater to drain away, and also provides a place for people to sit down and rest, while enjoying the magnificent views over the river.

The structure curves slightly around the space in front of it. The curve means that the countryside is framed from different angles through the gaps between the blocks. These spaces provide wonderful views of the surroundings, which are also reflected in the smooth, shiny paving stones.

Architects: Aranda, Pigem, and Vilalta
Location: Olot, Spain
Photography: Eugeni Pons

The roof grows progressively
thinner toward the eaves.

National Library of France | Dominique Perrault

Here the architect has worked on two apparently opposing scales: there is the monumentality of the whole building, symbolized by the towers; and there are enclosed spaces where the reader can experience a more intimate environment. The use of materials such as wood, which bears witness to the passing of time, is evidence of this intention. The central garden can be seen as the soul of the project, lending a sense of serenity to the whole complex.

Each part of the building is characterized by the use of specific materials. The towers are encased in glass, with a second skin of wood; the esplanade and railings are also in wood; and the four halls beneath the towers are lined in sheets of steel. The reading rooms have red carpets, wooden furniture, and ceilings formed by great nets of stainless steel suspended from the wall facing the garden. Here, the contrast in materials revolves around steel rather than glass.

The complex as a whole was built as a great public square, intended to play a full part in the urban landscape. The library's public facilities include reading rooms, galleries, research and audiovisual departments, an exhibition center, an auditorium, conference rooms, and restaurants.

Architect: Dominique Perrault

Location: Paris, France

Photography: Michel Denancé, George Fessy

Dominique Perrault's design is based on an apparent
paradox: the book stack
is on the upper floors
of the towers, where
there are the best views,
and the public reading
rooms on the lower floors.

View of one of the floors of the book stack. As can be seen,
the furniture is
in keeping with
the spirit of the
library as a whole.

Graz Airport | Riegler Riewe

At airports the activities of arriving, waiting, checking in, shopping, and eating all take place in a certain order, and this can be reflected in a particular sequence of spaces.

Small airports have the advantage that many of these activities can be carried out without losing sight of the final goal. The concept of having a series of spaces relies on how far one can see. One of the conditions of this brief was to create a single long space with plenty of overhead lighting, containing separate areas under one roof that would all be visible from any other part of the building. With this in mind, a wide interstice was cut into the structure to ensure unobstructed vision along the entire length of the building.

The redesign of the terminal was not limited only to improving the way it functioned, but also meant reinterpreting the whole interior with greater sensitivity, and adding new facades at the entrance and at the exits out to the runway.

The divisions between sections were carefully planned to soften the visual transition from one to the next, and to avoid the inconvenience of having too many signs.

Architects: Riegler Riewe
Location: Graz, Austria
Photography: Paul Ott

The facade facing the landing area is completely
encased in glass and
announces the name
of the airport in
big letters. It is
one enormous sign,
designed to be seen
from a long way off.

Kursaal Auditorium and Conference Center | Rafael Moneo

Few cities enjoy a setting as beautiful as that of San Sebastián in the Basque Country, in northern Spain. The site of these buildings is at the mouth of the River Urumea, and the auditorium and conference hall look like two rocks stranded in the estuary, as if not belonging to the city but forming part of the landscape. The galleries, meeting rooms, offices, and restaurant are all housed inside the base of the buildings, which provide a platform for the cubic blocks of the auditorium and conference hall.

The auditorium building floats inside a glass prism measuring 213 x 150 x 72 feet (65 x 46 x 22 meters), given movement by a slight incline toward the sea. Its asymmetry guides the audience toward the top floor, from where a wonderful view – with Mount Urgull and the sea in the background – can be seen through a highly unusual window. This window, piercing the double wall of the building, consists of a metal structure holding two glass blocks, which form the panes. It seals off the interior to protect its air conditioning and turns it into a neutral space, full of light, whose only other links with the outside world are the lobby windows, facing out to sea. The second building, which follows the same design, houses the conference hall.

Architect: Rafael Moneo

Location: San Sebastián, Spain

Photography: David Cardelús

At night the buildings, lit from inside, look like huge
lanterns beside the sea.

Alonso Ovallo Foundation Retreat | Glenda Kapstein, Osvaldo Muñoz

This center for meditation and prayer is situated on the coast of northern Chile. The natural landscape of desert, mountains, and sea is full of secluded places, ideal for contemplation. There are pockets of silence in the rugged terrain. In this project, distances from one place to another are also used to allow time for personal prayer and reflection. The buildings, walls, and even the plants have been arranged so as to insulate the center from the noise of the road.

The complex stretches from north to south, behind an outer wall that separates it from the freeway, and spreads out beside a large triangular piece of ground crossed by paths. It consists of a headquarters providing community services, an area of dormitory blocks, an oratory, and a chapel. The headquarters caters to the more public side of things: the main entrance, reception, and administration, meeting rooms, halls for various functions, dining rooms, and amphitheater. The oratory is a place for prayer and reflection, with no set hours or ritual.

The dormitories are on terraces facing the sea. To the west is the chapel, the only building set apart from the rest. At its entrance porch, paths from the oratory and the sacristy come together.

Architects: Glenda Kapstein, Osvaldo Muñoz
Location: Antofagasta, Chile
Photography: Glenda Kapstein

A cube forms a frame for the sky above the oratory, which is slightly sunk into the ground and acts as a stepping stone between the dormitories and the chapel. It is an outdoor place, with a pool, a fountain, and a flight of stairs.

Site plan

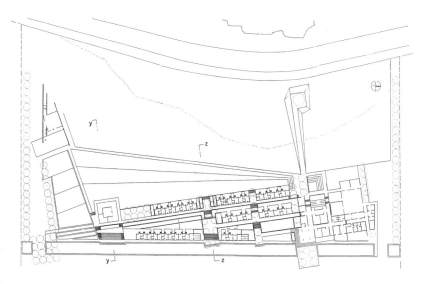

Wooden parasols are important in this place
of intense sunlight.

Civic Center in Ridaura | Aranda, Pigem, and Vilalta

The little village of Ridaura, in a valley in the province of Gerona, has 800 inhabitants. Until recently the only public buildings were the church and the town hall, as the school is in the ground floor of a house. Given this lack of public space, people wanted a new building for arts, leisure and sports activities. A site was chosen on the edge of the village, facing the church.

The aim of the project, almost an obsession for the young architects, was to respect the location, altering the environment without spoiling it. The challenge was to design an adaptable civic center that could be used for different activities and which would fit in to this particular landscape and community.

The building is a horizontal parallelepiped, which draws attention to the vertical line of the church. Constructed on a small scale, it is set sideways on the site to free up a square in front of it. There is a larger open area behind for games, dancing and sport. The open-air areas are linked by a series of deep, dark arcades, which form part of the building.

The originality of the Ridaura civic center lies in its sheer modernity, compared with the traditional agricultural nature of its surroundings.

Architects: Arnada, Pigem, and Vilalta
Location: Ridaura, Gerona, Spain
Photography: Eugeni Pons

Skylights, platforms, porticoes, and picture windows are
combined in a building
that fits in with its
surroundings and can
be used for a variety
of activities.

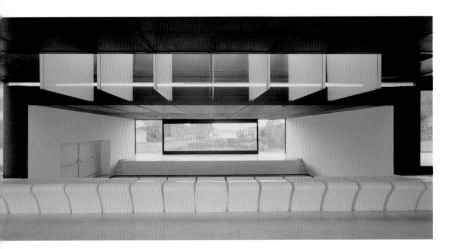

The glass walls and
skylights let in
plenty of natural
light to illuminate
the whole interior. Aranda, Pigem, and Vilalta insisted on a contemporary style.

Shopping Center, Hotel, and Homes | Bürgin, Niessen, Wentzlaff

To fit in with the urban environment, this project includes two towers: a five-story hotel with restaurant and a three-story residential block. The large shopping center occupies a lower, wider building between the two towers. The complex is built around a large paved area, where all public services are to be found. This is linked to the city's main shopping thoroughfare as well as providing access to the rest of the complex.

The lower part of the shopping center is covered in glass, which is dark green except for the windows, and it looks as if the entire surface is one flat sheet of glass. In contrast, the two blocks rising from this transparent base are covered in translucent glass. Behind this translucent surface you can just make out open spaces between solid blocks. Folding aluminum sheets provide protection from the sun.

It would have been difficult to subordinate the various different functions of this building to an austere, uniform design for the facades. As it is, the arrangement of translucent glass units and aluminum blinds in the facades follows a fairly flexible code, rather than a strict pattern.

Architects: Bürgin, Niessen, Wentzlaff
Location: Muttenz, Switzerland
Photography: Ruedi Walti

The complex is almost entirely covered in glass.
Three kinds of
material are used
in the facades:
dark green glass
for the base, which
seems to disappear;
white translucent
glass for the towers;
and a few small areas of
bare concrete wall which
blend in with this.

Signal Tower | Jacques Herzog, Pierre de Meuron, and Harry Gugger

The architecture of Herzog, de Meuron, and Gugger can be seen as an attempt to put art back into building design. They consider it essential to develop new, subversive strategies in their work, to contradict everyday perceptions and to ask questions rather than meeting unnecessary requirements.

This tall, copper edifice stands next to the 18th- and 19th-century walls of the Wolf-Gottesacker cemetery. It is a railroad control and signal tower, situated beside the train tracks and the shed for new locomotives. Its six floors are packed with sophisticated instruments and electronic equipment to control points and signals.

Bands of copper about 8 inches (20 centimeters) wide are wrapped around the concrete structure of the building. These strips open in places to let in daylight. When the strips are moved in order to be opened, lines of shadow that look like fish scales appear on the facades, and a change in texture comes over the surface of this striking, sealed-off building.

Architects: Jacques Herzog, Pierre de Meuron, and Harry Gugger

Location: Auf dem Wolf, Basel, Switzerland

Photography: Margherita Spiluttini

The building is a
highly unusual
landmark, a unique
signpost for a center
that transmits and
receives signals, and accumulates and organizes information.

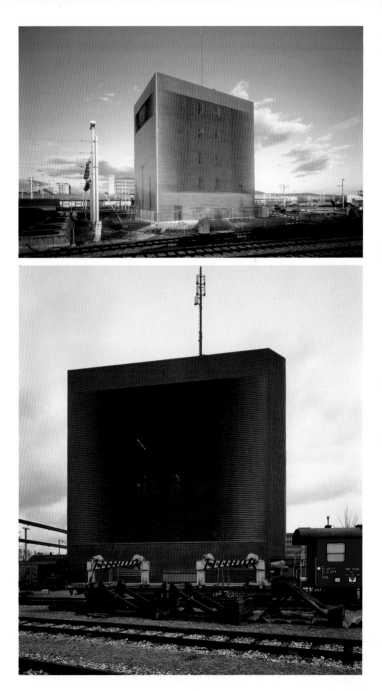

Interiors

Photo: Eugeni Pons

Photo: Eugeni Pons

Photo: Joan Mundó

Page 658: Rupert Steiner
Page 659: Emilio Conti

ment in Igualada. *Francesc Rifé* Minimalist Apartment. *John Pawson* Loft in Tur

oletto Camagna Marcante House 3R. *Hiroyuki Arima* Factory Conversion. *Simo*

der Associates Apartment in Stockholm. *Claesson Koivisto Rune Arkitektkont*

kerke House. *John Pawson* Converted Apartment. *Simon Conder* Home –

elona. *Franc Fernández* Apartment on the Thames. *Claudio Silvestrin* Apartment

e Carlo. *Claudio Lazzarini & Carl Pickering* Loft in London. *Stanton William*

ment in Vienna. *Eichinger oder Knechtl* Lofts in Vienna. *Lichtblau & Wagner* Loft

Mark Guard Loft in Milan. *Marco Savorelli* Adaptable Apartment. *Mark Guard* Whi

ment. *Frank Lupo & Daniel Rowen* Villa in Majorca. *Vincent van Duysen* House

dio Silvestrin Architects* House in Na Xemena. *Ramon Esteve* House in the Cerro

Santa. *Picado-De Blas-Delgado Architectural Studio* Studio Home in Islingto

so & St. John* House L. *Sauerbruch & Hutton* House K in K. *Heinz & Nikolau*

efeld House M. *Kazuyo Sejima & Ryue Nishizawa* Refurbishment and Extension of

e. *Josep Llobet* House 2/5. *Shigeru Ban* House H. *Sauerbruch & Hutton* Ibor

e. *Xavier Llobet/Xavier Ballarín* Fausto Santini in Düsseldorf. *Antonio Citterio*

ers Giorgio Armani in New York. *Peter Marino* Julie Sohn in Barcelona. *Conrad*

sco & Carlos Tejada* Jigsaw in London. *John Pawson* Giorgio Armani in Par

dio Silvestrin Architects* Principe Boutique. *Antonio Citterio & Partners* Fendi

e. *Claudio Lazzarini & Carl Pickering* Louis Vuitton in Paris. *Peter Marino*

ciates* Bottega Veneta. *François de Menil* Antonio Pernas in Barcelona. *Iago Sea*

aeltz. *Shigeru Uchida* Calvin Klein in New York. *John Pawson* Jeweler's in Munic

au & Kindelbacher* Bulthaup Showroom in Barcelona. *Arturo Frediani* Elevation Salo

é. Petersen & Verwers Hotel Ace. *Eric Hentz/Mallet* Nil Bar and Restaurant. *Claud*

arini & Carl Pickering* Casa Pilar Café-Bar. *A-cero Architects* Nodo Restaurant. *Da*

as/Varis Architects* One Happy Cloud Restaurant. *Claesson Koivisto Run*

ektkontor* El Japonés Restaurant. *López & Tarruella* Wagamama Restaurant. *Dav*

perfield Architects* No Picnic Office. *Claesson Koivisto Rune Arkitektkontor* Offic

fé i Associats. *Francesc Rifé* Recoletos Publishing House. *Wortmann Bañare*

tects Osho International Offices. *Daniel Rowen* Finance Office. *Wortmann Bañare*

tects Office of GCA Architects. *GCA Architects* Faculty of Law. *Aranda, Pigem, an*

a Primary School in Vienna. *Götz/Manahl* New World School. *Adolf Krischani*

Apartment in Igualada | Francesc Rifé

This home is divided into two main sections, one for day and one for night, separated by the entrance hall and front door. The daytime areas adjoin the main facade, which receives the most light, and include a living room, dining room, and terrace. The kitchen faces the entrance and can be shut off behind a large sliding door.

The central hall, lined with maple storage units, links the two parts of the apartment and acts as the hub of the whole space. A long, indirectly lit niche runs across the apartment and holds storage for domestic items.

The furniture in the dining room and kitchen has been made to measure. The dining table can be extended by 3 feet (1 meter), using an internal mechanism, and has two drawers in the ends. The kitchen, all in bone white, is divided into two parts, one for cooking and one for eating. The U-shaped counter allows the glass table to link the two areas. All fittings, gadgets, and handles are in matt stainless steel.

The nocturnal area includes two bedrooms, a study, a bathroom, and the master bedroom. You enter the master bedroom through a door in the outer paneling, passing a dressing room and bathroom on the way.

Architect: Francesc Rifé

Location: Igualada, Barcelona, Spain

Photography: Joan Mundó

Access to the apartment is from a vestibule
with elevators and
stairs. The front
door and the wall
facing the lift
are made of maple
wood, whose warm
tone contrasts with
the stainless steel.

The hall is
lined in maple
wood, incorporating
doors, closets, and cupboards.

Minimalist Apartment | John Pawson

There are different kinds of minimalism. There are the Mediterranean architects who have continued to distill the legacy of the Modern Movement and popular tradition; then, there is the Calvinist austerity of Central European architecture; finally, there is contemporary Japanese architecture, which is a reinterpretation of spiritualism. It is this last school that influenced British architect John Pawson when he visited the Far East.

Pawson has shown that well-designed, powerful and convincing buildings can be made with few gestures, without needing adornment or accessories to make sense.

The brief for this project included private living quarters and an open-plan space for art exhibitions. The gallery, library, and living rooms are at the front of the apartment. The dining room and kitchen are at the back, separated by a wall measuring 98 feet (30 meters) in length.

The design consists of a series of monumental walls, which split off the smaller private living spaces. The sober texture and bone-colored tones of the walls create a solemn but warm ambience. The partitions are bathed in an even light, with the light sources hidden to avoid glare.

Architect: John Pawson

Location: London, United Kingdom

Photography: Richard Glover

All the walls, like the furniture, are white, and
subtly but clearly
separated from the
pale wooden floor,
as though they
were floating.

Loft in Turin | Camoletto Camagna Marcante

This was an uninhabited loft on the fourth floor of an 18th-century building in the baroque center of Turin. It measures 300 square feet (90 square meters) and is on two levels. The project was commissioned by a young couple, one employed in the motor trade and one in avant-garde fashion. Despite the limited area available the architect succeeded in creating a home that makes highly organized use of the space and where every function has its place.

On the first level there are two bedrooms, each with its own bathroom, and a utility room. A staircase seems to float upward from the front door, where the roof is at its lowest. The upper level is for daytime use, and has a kitchen, pantry, living area and dining area. All these, except the pantry, are together in one open-plan room, which helps give the apartment a sense of spaciousness. The kitchen is defined by different flooring and by a gentler slope in the ceiling. The original central supporting wall has been replaced by a thick double wall of translucent glass, which acts as a vehicle for both natural and artificial light, and communicates, both horizontally and vertically, between the main rooms.

Architect: Camoletto Camagna Marcante
Location: Turin, Italy
Photography: Emilio Conti

Lower floor

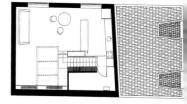

Upper floor

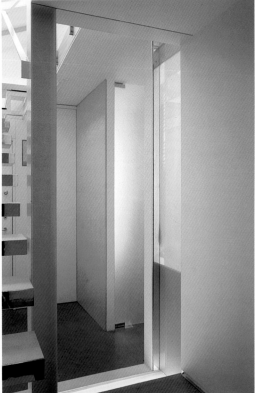

The conversion of the apartment was part of a renovation program for the whole building. The brick supporting walls and wooden roof were partly replaced by a metal structure.

The reduced size of the metal roof structure, compared with the original wooden one, ensures that the maximum space possible is available for the living space on the top floor.

House 3R | Hiroyuki Arima

A small block of duplex apartments, 20 years old, has been refurbished to create lighter, more pleasant, and more spacious places to live. The external appearance of the building was left unchanged, any such alteration having been ruled out at the planning stage. The block is on a site that slopes northward, beside a raised road. A stairway leads down from the road to the entrance, at ground level.

This apartment has been redesigned as one continuous space, with no fixed partitions separating the rooms. Its name, 3R, refers to three mobile panels near the entrance. These can be arranged at different angles to modify the space in any number of ways, according to taste. The walls, floors, and ceilings are painted white so as to make the most of the poor natural light from the north. The rooms flow into each other on both floors, which are linked by a staircase. The original outer windows have been covered with sheets of translucent plastic, leaving small spaces that can be used for storage, for books, or even as a belvedere looking onto the garden.

Architect: Hiroyuki Arima
Location: Fukuoka, Japan
Photography: Okamoto

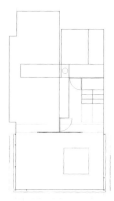

Ground floor

Upper floor

The interior partitions were removed to make a larger, freer space. Translucent screens filter the light to create an ethereal atmosphere without shadows, and where darkness steals in very gradually.

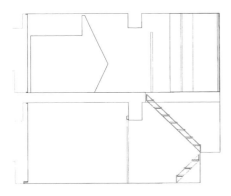

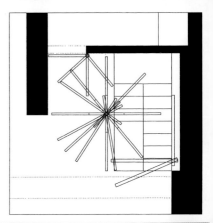

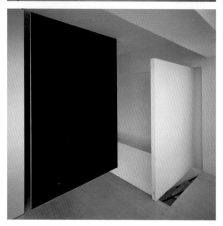

Factory Conversion | Simon Conder Associates

The need for a free, unconfined space was the chief priority in this design for an old factory. The client, a painter who lives in Kent, wanted an apartment in London as a base from which to explore the city's artistic life.

In making use of this area measuring 1250 square feet (116 square meters), the aim was to stress the sense of light and openness that characterized the original building. The idea was therefore to avoid partitioning the space, but without impairing its ability to function efficiently.

It was decided, given the lack of room available, to keep the whole place open in plan, though the staircase visually separates the sleeping from the living area. The main space features three vertical elements: the stainless-steel kitchen, and two cylinders containing the shower and a bathroom. The party walls serve many purposes: along them are installed clothes closets, plumbing, wiring, and even a foldaway bed for guests, along with their own bathroom.

The key to these English architects' success lies in doing away with all surface ornament, which would have distracted from the clarity of the design. Technical clutter is hidden away in ceilings, cupboards, and furniture. In this way even individual lights are rendered unnecessary.

Architects: Simon Conder Associates
Location: London, United Kingdom
Photography: Simon Archer

The central section of the apartment is two stories high, allowing access to a terrace on the top floor. The studio, facing toward London's West End, has views out over the city to the south and west. The materials used create a minimalist ambience. The kitchen, staircase, and structure of the glassed-in gallery are of stainless steel. The floor, under which the heating is housed, is of white oak.

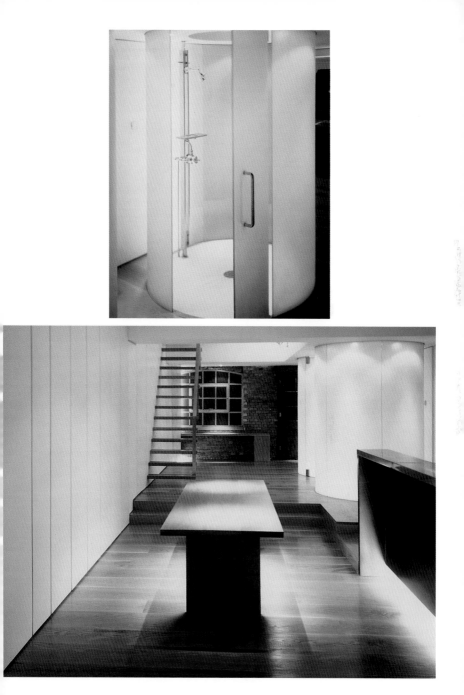

Apartment in Stockholm | Claesson Koivisto Rune Arkitektkontor

This project was commissioned by the building firm PEAB, who asked for a design for the interior of a show apartment in a building by the architect Jacques Sandjian, incorporating a studio and workshop into the living space. The architects Claesson, Koivisto, and Rune invented a client, a textile designer called Pia Wallén, partly because she shared their non-materialist values, such as a belief in visual, spatial, and spiritual freedom and a love of contemplation, and partly because she had once employed them.

The apartment is on two levels, linked by stairs. Various alterations were made to the original design: most of the internal partitions were removed, some doors were turned into sliding ones, and openings were made in walls to create views along and across the whole space.

All the furniture, the floors, and the stairs are in pale wood. These harmonize with the white walls, which are set off by a few careful touches of color here and there in the upholstery, on a sliding door, or on a wall.

Architects: Claesson Koivisto Rune Arkitektkontor
Location: Stockholm, Sweden
Photography: Åke Eison Lindman

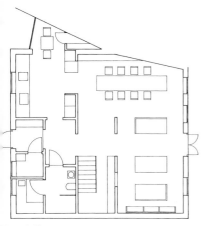

Ground floor

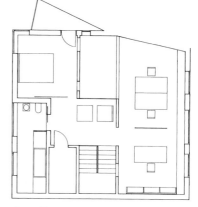

Upper floor

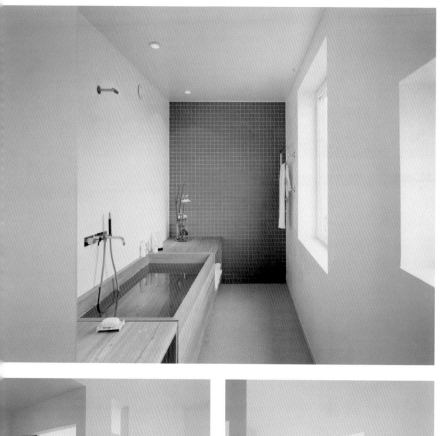

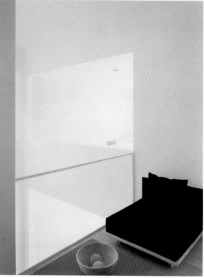

Moerkerke House | John Pawson

Here a Victorian apartment has been converted into a home for three people. The kitchen bathroom, and stairs were moved to make better use of limited space. The lower floor, containing the kitchen, living room, and dining room, has been opened out as much as possible to form one large space, which can be subdivided if necessary.

Two elements have been added to modify the proportions of the interior space and make room for domestic necessities: a chimney wall, containing a staircase, and a partition to close off the kitchen, with a stainless-steel smoke extractor. A skylight pours light down onto the steps of the staircase, which fits snugly into the chimney wall. The floors on both levels are of cherry wood and the walls are painted in soothing white. The windows are hung with white fabric, which filters the light and shuts out the outside world. A simple table with six chairs by Wegner and two pairs of armchairs by Christian Liagre are the only visible furniture.

Architect: John Pawson

Location: London, United Kingdom

Photography: Richard Glover

The partitions hover slightly above floor level, as light and subtle as curtains. Natural light plays an important role in this building. All the windows are covered in white fabric, providing diffuse light that is reflected off the walls with hardly a shadow. This creates an almost unreal sensation of pure, abstract space.

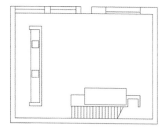

Ground floor

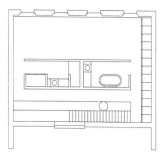

Upper floor

Converted Apartment | Simon Conder

An old fire station in West London has been turned into a home for a couple: a musician and a chef. The building was long and narrow, and there were not enough windows to light the whole space naturally. To let daylight into the lower levels, the architect opted for a metal and glass structure in the roof. This glass roof can be opened in summer, turning the space below it into a pleasant terrace.

The partitions dividing up the interior on all three floors were removed, and a stone stairway was built up one of the side walls, leading from the entrance at street level all the way to the conservatory at the top. On the first floor are the hall, the main bedroom with en suite bathroom, two smaller bedrooms, and another bathroom. On the second floor the dining room, kitchen, and living room share one large open space. Here a wooden piece of furniture housing a CD collection also serves as a desk.

The architect has designed much of the furniture so that it fits into the structure of the house: the bed in the main bedroom, the bathtub, the fitted kitchen, and the wooden banister rail.

Architect: Simon Conder

Location: London, United Kingdom

Photography: Chris Gascoigne/View

Cutaway section

Light floods down into the kitchen-
dining area
between the
wooden slats of
the ceiling, from
the glass-covered
terrace above.

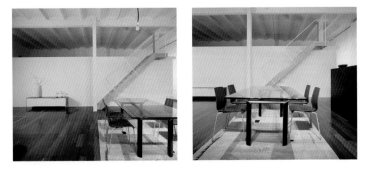

Home in Barcelona | Franc Fernández

Here an old factory warehouse has been converted for residential use. Keeping the building at its original height of 15 feet (4.5 meters) helped preserve its industrial character and gave the new homes a distinctive quality.

This apartment has the advantage of being in a corner of the building, so that it has ample natural light. Its owner, an actress, was looking for somewhere large and flexible. Since the apartment was to be used for rehearsals and performance, space, light, and versatility were priorities.

The existing structure was preserved, and the metal girders and pillars, the tiled, fluted ceilings, and even the original large windows were retained. The space was divided into two parts, one combining the kitchen, dining room, and living room, the other containing the bedroom, bathroom, toilet, and study. The first, more public, area has kept the original high ceiling and receives most of the light. The second is divided by a platform, which gives the more private rooms a secluded, intimate feel. Just above this, a space 5 feet (1.5 meters) high houses the library.

Architect: Franc Fernández
Location: Barcelona, Spain
Photography: Joan Mundó

Floor plan

The unit containing the bedroom, bathroom, toilet, and study is lined in water-resistant, varnished beechwood. Mirrors magnify the space in the bathroom. To take up as little space as possible, the rooms are connected by sliding doors, some of them in translucent glass.

In this apartment Franc Fernández has used the few resources at his disposal to find a wealth of architectural solutions.

Apartment on the Thames | Claudio Silvestrin

This converted apartment, on the bank of the River Thames in London, is in a concrete and glass building designed by Sir Norman Foster in the late 1980s. It is on the fourth floor, its facades are oriented toward north, west, and south, and it has fine views over the river and surrounding city.

The first decision was to open a wide corridor all along the inner wall of the apartment, to allow movement through it lengthwise. A curved screen of translucent glass from floor to ceiling separates the kitchen – which has no door – and the bedroom area from the more public spaces such as the living room and study. Interestingly, this screen reveals as much as it shuts off, since shadows and silhouettes of objects on both sides appear on its surface, uniting the two.

Silvestrin's handling of light in this piece of work is decidedly poetic. To the south and west he softens it with translucent hangings, then diffuses it through the curved glass screen, making this solid object appear almost liquid. The same ambiguity is repeated in the floor, paved throughout in huge slabs of Tuscan stone, which echo the calm, liquid gray of the Thames.

Architect: Claudio Silvestrin
Location: London, United Kingdom
Photography: Claudio Silvestrin Architects

In a minimalist attempt to keep everyday domestic
necessities out of sight,
there are long cupboards
from floor to ceiling,
like walls or columns.

It may seem a strange
idea to keep books in
closed cabinets, but
in this particular
private domain, minimalist
dogma is perfectly in tune with the clients' wishes.

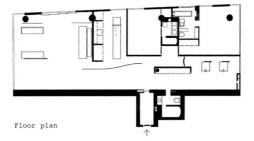

Floor plan

Silvestrin emphasizes the nature of each space and softens any excesses by the way he handles light and form. Having freed the space of all obstructions except for the structural pillars, he sets about expanding and unifying it both physically and visually.

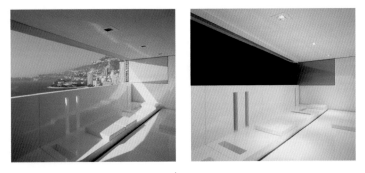

Apartment in Monte Carlo | Claudio Lazzarini & Carl Pickering

This apartment, on the 14th floor of the Mirabeau skyscraper, was made by joining together two apartments that are divided by a supporting wall of reinforced concrete.

The client is a businessman who spends only part of his week in Monte Carlo and nearly always eats out. The idea was to create a suite with a terrace for enjoyable breakfasts and aperitifs at sundown.

The design was for a single, fluid space to make the most of the superb views out to sea. The supporting wall that divides the apartment lengthwise was disguised with mirrors, glass blocks allowing you to see from one side to the other, and openings in stainless steel.

The bathrooms, kitchen, and closets are conceived as independent items standing in a single space. The terrace, designed like the deck of a ship, is a continuation of the interior.

The three-dimensional partitions can be moved around on wheels to alter the way the space is divided, and have swiveling panels that can be left open where desired.

Architects: Claudio Lazzarini & Carl Pickering
Location: Monte Carlo, Monaco
Photography: Matteo Piazza

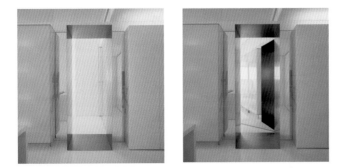

The shower is behind the bed, looking out to sea through a glass screen.
The play of
reflections on
shiny surfaces,
transparent glass,
and mirrors fills
the space with
light.
The architects
also designed some
of the furniture:
the tables, bed,
and kitchen units.

Loft in London | Stanton Williams

The architect was asked to turn the loft of an old factory building in London into a working and living space. The client, a freelance designer, wanted a main living area that he could also use for meetings with his clients without feeling inhibited by a domestic atmosphere.

Enormous sliding windows that stretch from floor to ceiling open onto a secluded, south-facing terrace. The north-facing windows are smaller, so that the kitchen has a solid backdrop. The kitchen units and appliances are tucked discreetly into a low, compact block, which blends into the space. The slightly raised kitchen floor is of cedar wood.

Skylights have been positioned so as to light particular areas and emphasize some of the vertical planes. Wood has been used for the floors and the fixed and sliding partitions. The walls, ceilings, and alcoves are plastered; and the doors are made of painted wooden planks. The other materials used in the interior are stainless steel and translucent glass.

Architect: Stanton Williams
Location: London, United Kingdom
Photography: Chris Gascoigne/View

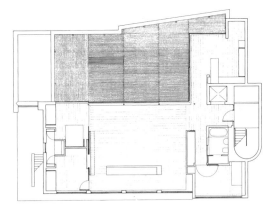

Floor plan

Apartment in Vienna | Eichinger oder Knechtl

A former laundry in an attic has been converted into this apartment, which measures 380 square feet (35 square meters). Apart from the bedroom, measuring 160 square feet (15 square meters), everything is contained in a single space.

The architects removed a partition wall, covered the roof beams with metal sheets and plasterboard, and replaced part of the outer wall with a large glass window in two sections.

Entering through a heavy, armored door, you find a cabinet covered in semi-transparent wire mesh, which acts as a partition. At night this is lit from the inside to become a huge lantern reaching up to the ceiling. It contains the washing machine and controls for the windows, lighting, and heating.

The stainless-steel door of the bathroom closes to reveal a passage leading to the kitchen, at the rear of the apartment. The kitchen is fitted into an oak unit that runs to the outer wall, beyond which it becomes a block of concrete containing a small herb garden.

The great window is electrically operated. The top part swings out to a height of 7 feet (2.10 meters), and the lower part can slide farther out, along the block that runs out from the kitchen unit, to form a balcony for additional space.

Architects: Eichinger oder Knechtl
Location: Vienna, Austria
Photography: Margherita Spiluttini

A wire-mesh screen, like a curtain, closes to form a shower unit. The controls are built into a metal pillar and the floor is
made of oak. When the screen
is drawn back, the shower and
toilet are completely hidden.

Lofts in Vienna | Lichtblau & Wagner

This loft conversion is remarkable for its use of energy-saving devices that until now have only been applied to other fields of architecture. Most residential design concentrates on functional and aesthetic matters, but Lichtblau & Wagner have tried to introduce ways of saving both energy and money.

With this in mind, they have rejected superficial luxuries such as marble baths, outdoor terraces, and outsized entrances, to focus on a flexible design that saves energy and space, and keeps costs down.

The design consists of four basic units of 500 square feet (50 square meters) each, arranged two by two, with an extra space that can easily be added to one apartment or the other by relocating the partitions. Communal areas house a storeroom, a laundry, and a hall for meetings or parties, which supplements the limited space in the studios.

Maximum use has been made of the space, in an efficient layout with reduced areas for circulation. The rooms can be used for many different purposes. The space beneath the windows, for example, can serve as a balcony, gallery, or conservatory.

Architects: Lichtblau & Wagner

Location: Vienna, Austria

Photography: Andreas Wagner,
Margherita Spiluttini

The elimination of internal walls reduces building costs. All pipes and cables are installed under the floor, so that there is no need to bore holes in the partitions. The kitchen and bathroom units can be dismantled and, since they are connected to the water supply by holes in the floor, it is possible to move them around or even remove them altogether.

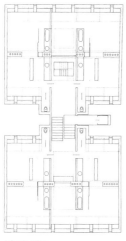

Floor plan

Lichtblau & Wagner
see bathrooms not as
enclosed rooms but
as part of the
living space, with natural light and a view.

Loft in Paris | Mark Guard

The client is the owner of this small but remarkable loft on the roof of a 1930s apartment block in Paris.

In only 345 square feet (32 square meters) of space, he wanted to have a separate bedroom and to be able to put up visiting friends and relatives.

The solution was found with the aid of three box-like units that can be arranged at will, one hinged door and several sliding ones. The apartment is now completely adaptable. The bedroom can form part of the main space or be separated from it. The bathroom can be entered directly from the bedroom or connected to the living room, where there is a sofa bed for guests.

The boxes contain the washing machine, refrigerator, television, and a towel cupboard, which is revealed when the bathroom door is closed. The cooker fits into a stainless-steel unit and is separated from the bathroom only by a pane of glass, which turns opaque when a device is triggered by the bathroom door closing.

The western wall of the apartment was replaced by a transparent, removable door, and a glass canopy that makes it possible to leave the doors open when it rains in summer.

Architect: Mark Guard

Location: Paris, France

Photography: Jacques Crenn

The stone floor continues out onto the terrace, from where there is a wonderful view of the historic center of Paris.

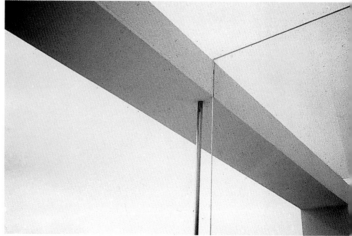

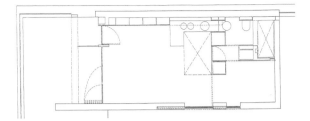

Floor plan

High-tech wizardry allows the client to turn on the heating and hot water with a phone call from his London home before he arrives in Paris.

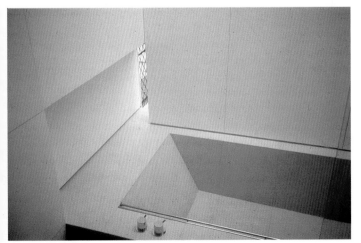

Loft in Milan | Marco Savorelli

An old loft in the historic center of Milan has been converted into a modern apartment measuring about 970 square feet (90 square meters). The layout was planned with no reference to the original, and with the general idea of combining everything in one space and avoiding internal doors and partitions. The use of the same dark wooden flooring throughout also contributes to the unity of the space, and contrasts crisply with the white of the walls and sloping ceilings.

Both client and architect aimed to start from scratch, working in the abstract, in the apartment, to develop their new design. Taking into account the slope of the roof, they placed the main passageway at its highest point, down the center. Spaces for restful activities were arranged around the perimeter.

Functional elements such as the bathroom, kitchen, and closets are housed in monolithic blocks, whose simple shape gives them authority and which inspire new ways of looking at space. These functional blocks, stripped of their obvious purpose, hover between irony and provocation. The entrance leads into the living room, and the bedroom merges into the bathroom and kitchen in the center of the apartment.

Architect: Marco Savorelli
Location: Milan, Italy
Photography: Matteo Piazza

The décor is plain and monastic. Being able to see the entire space from almost anywhere in the apartment gives it a sense of peace and fluidity.

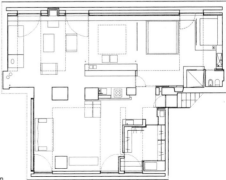

Floor plan

Adaptable Apartment | Mark Guard

This design explores the potential for adaptability and maximum use of space in

Floor plan

Architect: Mark Guard

Location: London, United Kingdom

Photography: Alan Williams

a small apartment. The flat can have either one or two bedrooms, or none, or be turned into one large workspace. The beds for both the main bedroom and the guestroom are kept in two independent box-like units. A third box holds a bathroom and toilet. The doors of these boxes form the sliding partitions of the bedrooms.

A large storage wall holds the television, the sound system, the kitchen, pantry, and washing machine, a clothes closet for the main bedroom, and other useful items.

Between the three boxes, centered on the bathroom, there is a large stainless-steel table, 20 feet (6 meters) long. The bathtub is next to this table, separated from it only by a pane of special glass whose opacity can be adjusted at the touch of a button. When the bedrooms are folded away into their boxes, the total space measures 18 x 50 feet (5.5 x 15 meters). The bathroom stands free of the outer walls, an abstract, striking object like a sculpture. The views from and through it add another visual dimension to the apartment.

White Apartment | Frank Lupo & Daniel Rowen

This design turned two traditional apartments in Park Avenue into one ethereal space, an effect that is emphasized by the removal of some of the windows and the arrangement of translucent screens. When the client expressed his appreciation of the play of light on the various surfaces of the walls, floors, and ceilings, it was decided to keep the whole place empty of furniture.

The wooden floor, the walls, and the ceilings are all painted white. The partitions barely touch the floor, creating the impression that they are not fixed and could be moved. Sliding doors that stretch from floor to ceiling run on an embedded rail, so that only the flat planes of the doors are visible. The screens of semi-transparent white fabric, also fitted invisibly, filter the light and isolate the space from the outside world.

The minimalist aesthetic of the apartment creates a contemplative ambience, in stark contrast with the lively atmosphere of the heart of Manhattan.

Architects: Frank Lupo & Daniel Rowen
Location: New York, USA
Photography: Michael Moran

The isolation and extreme simplicity of this design allows the occupant to
explore his or her senses
without any distraction.
This is a place to listen
to the light, watch the
silence, and dream.

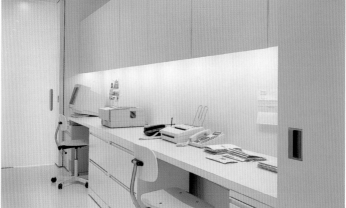

Villa in Majorca | Vincent van Duysen

This project involved converting a traditional old house in inland Majorca. The facades, including those of the two adjacent buildings (the caretaker's house and the owner's office), were kept intact. Inside, however, the aim was to create a restrained and highly contemporary atmosphere.

Extensive wooden fencing divides the house from the caretaker's and encloses a large yet intimate courtyard. The architect was also responsible for designing the garden, which he linked to the house by using the same paving for both: a combination of concrete and local stone. An alcove containing a great stone sink, hewn from a single slab, adds a theatrical touch here.

The house is in the same vein. The furniture, carefully designed for each room, is made from simple shapes with plain surfaces, to create an almost monastic effect. Wood, stone, ceramics, and marble are sensitively combined in an elegant and relaxed ensemble. The entrance hall is an empty space, whose wood-paneled walls conceal a door to the guest bathroom. The hall leads into the kitchen-dining room and, via the stairs, to the bedrooms on the upper floor.

Architect: Vincent van Duysen

Location: Majorca, Spain

Photography: Alberto Emanuele Piovano

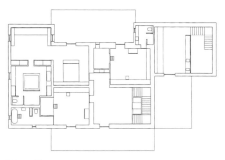

Upper floor

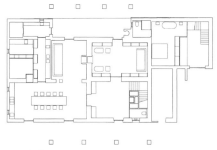

Ground floor

A few strategically placed elements stand out against
the background of
floors in calm
shades of white.

House B | Claudio Silvestrin Architects

The project here was to refurbish an 8,600 square-foot (800 square-meter) farmhouse on the outskirts of a small village halfway between Nice and Aix-en-Provence. During the 17th century the building served as a staging post for monks and pilgrims on their way to Avignon along the old Roman road.

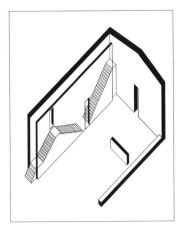

Axonometric projection

The building is on two floors, and divided lengthwise by a supporting wall. The new home was designed around these existing features. It is peaceful and austere, with no superfluous adornment, but full of spiritual vitality.

The chief material is stone, which has been used for all the floors and much of the furniture. All the walls are plastered and painted white. There are two sets of doors in the main facade, each one leading to different rooms. The heavy doors of the old barn open inward to reveal a vast space used as a living room and reception area.

The staircase, which acts as a huge, broad partition, runs the entire length of the house and leads to all the rooms: first to the guestrooms, then to the drawing room, and finally to the principal bedroom area. The way the stairs have been placed between two thick walls gives this simple space an almost cathedral-like grandeur.

Architects: Claudio Silvestrin Architects

Location: Provence, France

Photography: Claudio Silvestrin Architects

Everything in the master suite is made of stone, including the two washbowls
cut into the wall,
a monolithic shower,
and an oval bathtub,
which displays all the
sensual charms of stone.

House in Na Xemena | Ramon Esteve

Working in the magnificent natural surroundings of Na Xemena, in northeastern Ibiza, demands sensitivity and respect for such harmony and grandeur. Establishing a relationship between a building and the scenery around it is one of the most exciting challenges of architecture.

From the first stages of planning to choosing materials and colors, the shapes and other elements of the building were put together organically, though logically, without adhering to a rigid geometric layout. The house has been designed to be able to grow, along the lines set down in the original nucleus. The various blocks making up the interior have been added as a sequence of spaces that increase proportionally in size.

The complex is built on rocky ground, and forms a compact, simple whole, following the contours of the cliff. From the outside, the gently shelving arrangement of the terraces and swimming pool leads the eye up to the sturdy shape of the house at the top. It does not clamor for attention, but rather fits gracefully and naturally into the landscape.

Architect: Ramon Esteve
Location: Ibiza, Spain
Photography: Ramon Esteve

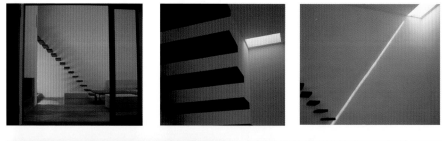

The staircase is one of the key
features of
the interior.

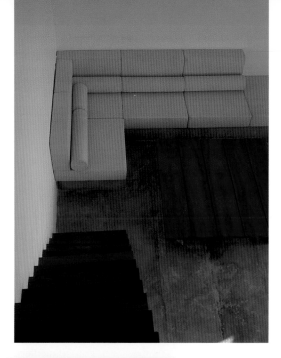

House in the Cerros de la Santa | Picado-De Blas-Delgado Architectural Studio

This country house was planned and built on a very limited budget. The main aim was to make the most of the wonderful views over the Vera valley. A large opening was therefore made to face west, where the sun sets behind a medieval castle on a hilltop half a mile (1 kilometer) away. After studying the site, the architects drew up a two-tier plan, consisting on the one hand of a huge central common area, and on the other of rooms that both serve and make sense of it.

The central living space, 14 feet (4.2 meters) high, is the route to all other areas. It contains the main supporting walls and also boasts the magnificent view already mentioned. The east-west axis, so apparent in the plans, is softened here by lower extensions on all sides, which also make the relationship between interior and exterior more fluid. The natural light coming in from these outer areas accentuates the effect. Seen from the outside, the arrangement of the blocks reflects the internal structure of concrete ceilings and supporting walls.

To make it blend in more with its surroundings, the building is painted in shades of brownish green, melting unnoticed into the countryside.

Architects: Picado-De Blas-Delgado
Architectural Studio
Location: Cáceres, Spain
Photography: Eugeni Pons

Studio Home in Islington | Caruso & St. John

Adam Caruso and Peter St. John have turned a two-story former warehouse in Islington, North London, into a combined home and studio. The warehouse was a rectangle measuring 15 feet (4.7 meters) across the front and 32 feet (9.8 meters) deep, which gave a usable surface area of about 480 square feet (45 square meters) on each floor. It had brick walls and wooden beams, and the space was completely open, with no partitions or freestanding pillars.

The idea of the design was to respect the existing building and to fill the interior with natural light.

There were hardly any windows, so the architects decided to replace the original facade with a glass wall, double-glazed to keep heat in and sound out. The panes are translucent, letting in the light but shutting out the view. They act like a screen of silk or tissue paper: by day the facade is completely sealed off, as though covered in sheet metal; at night it becomes a lantern illuminating the street.

The facade is divided into horizontal bands of varying width, outlined by the metal strips holding the panes of glass.

Architects: Caruso & St. John
Location: London, United Kingdom
Photography: Hélène Binet

First floor

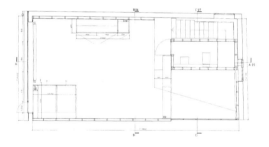

Ground floor

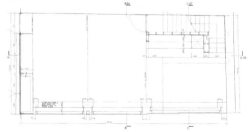

The rough surfaces of the old
warehouse have not
been disguised;
on the contrary,
the materials used
for the new features
have been adapted to
fit in with the old.
The final result is
an honest, austere,
and inward-looking space.

House L | Sauerbruch & Hutton

Sauerbruch & Hutton had the task of converting this conventional Victorian terraced house in London. They organized the building – 1,800 square feet (170 square meters) of space over four floors – to house offices on the first two floors and living quarters on the other two. On this occasion the clients were the architects themselves.

The process of conversion showed how the concept of space – and people's whole outlook – evolved between Victorian times and the early 1990s. During the second half of the 19th century, buildings would be divided up into many enclosed, inward-looking rooms. At the end of the 20th century, on the other hand, the trend was to create clear, open, bright, and practical spaces, often playing with the visual and physical relationship between different parts of a design and between the whole and its surroundings.

A climb upstairs, during which you are bombarded with sensations of increasing intensity, culminates on the fourth floor at the top, where all partitions have been removed to open up the entire space. Living room, dining room, and kitchen are all combined into one.

Architects: Sauerbruch & Hutton

Location: London, United Kingdom

Photograhy: Michael Claus, Katsuhisa Kida, Hélène Binet, Charlie Stebbings

The decision to open up the roof of the building gives it a unique and wonderful view of the ever-changing London sky. The sky is like an extension of the home, a kind of private garden. By day the light pours in, either directly or filtered through hangings. After dark a beam of artificial light shines out from this top floor and loses itself in the night.

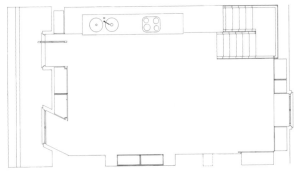

Top floor

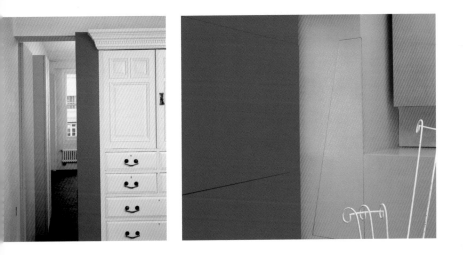

House K in K | Heinz & Nikolaus Bienefeld

This L-shaped house has been reorganized to make better use of the space. Stairs near the front door lead to the upper floor, which was originally dominated by four rectangular columns supporting a skylight. The entrance has been altered to improve the lighting on the stairs, and the columns have been replaced by a metal structure holding the skylight from above. Now, the wide, clearly lit staircase is the dominant feature of this space.

In the dining room, a large window of insulating glass has replaced a wall facing the house next door. This opened up and let light into a relatively dark room. The most noteworthy features in this house are unusual touches such as the metal surface on the ground floor or the wooden furniture designed by the architect himself. Most striking of all is the use of color, especially on the ground floor. Heinz Bienefeld wanted to achieve the effect of an abstract painting in architecture, and to handle the color distinctively. He worked with his son Nikolaus, a painter and sculptor whose style is minimalist and three-dimensional. The result is a delicate yet unsentimental color scheme.

Architects: Heinz & Nikolaus Bienefeld

Photography: Lukas Roth Architekturfotografie

In the dining room, a wall facing the neighboring
house was replaced
with a large window
of insulating glass.

The wooden furniture was
designed by the
architect himself.

House M | Kazuyo Sejima and Ryue Nishizawa

This house is in a residential neighborhood of large homes in central Tokyo, where development has accelerated in recent years. The lots usually measure about 2,150 square feet (200 square meters). Many of the houses in this street have big windows on their south-facing facade, but, since this is also the side that faces the street, the curtains are often drawn and the houses hidden behind tall fences. Given these circumstances the plan was to bring the outdoors indoors, while still protecting the privacy of the space.

The clients' requirements included two studies, a guestroom, two bathrooms, parking space for two cars, a room for their future child, and a large room for parties.

The whole site was excavated to put the house on a lower level than the street and surrounding buildings. Some rooms, such as the main bedroom, guestroom, and parking space, are at street level. The dining room, a study, and other open spaces were laid out on the lower floor, interspersed with courtyards to let in the light. From here the noise of the street sounds very far away, and the desired seclusion and privacy were thus achieved.

Architects: Kazuyo Sejima and Ryue Nishizawa
Location: Tokyo, Japan
Photography: Shinkenchiku-Sha

Large windows
surround the
inner courtyard
and let in natural light, filtered through fine shutters.

Refurbishment and Extension of a House | Josep Llobet

This house is near the old quarter of a small town in the Spanish province of Gerona. The original layout of its rooms was confusing, so the aim was to make the place more convenient for daily living by extending the ground floor and reorganizing the existing space.

The site is long and narrow, with a street at each end. The building itself is right on the main street. The improvements involved changing the position of some walls, making a large opening, and installing a skylight. These three steps redefined the functions of the kitchen, pantry, laundry space, and bathroom. Most of the life of the house revolves around the living room and dining room, which share a single space divided by a fireplace. These elements are arranged around a central marble wall.

The flow of movement along the length of the house is only interrupted by this marble wall, which turns the family living areas into a quiet retreat. The rear facade is extremely simple, and faces a narrow lane in the middle of town.

Architect: Josep Llobet
Location: Vidreres, Spain
Photography: Josep Llobet, Eugeni Pons

The service areas
are compact and
enclosed, while
the living spaces
are flowing and
open. Next to the
front door, facing
the street, are
two rooms slightly
set apart from the
rest: a workshop and a sewing room.

Ground-floor plan

House 2/5 | Shigeru Ban

House 2/5 is one of a series of experimental buildings based on the exploration of space and light in relation to the surroundings. Designed for intrepid clients, each prototype aims to provide a housing solution for all aspects of domestic life.

The objective in this house, on the outskirts of the city, was to create a private space, insulated from the noise and pollution of its urban surroundings. Incorporating a modified version of a traditional domestic inner courtyard, Ban divided the total area into five equal zones that alternate interior spaces with gardens and terraces.

The house is bordered to the east and west by concrete walls two stories high. To the north a thick PVC barrier guards its privacy. Covering the facade facing the street is a screen of folded and perforated aluminum, through which one can make out the ramp leading to the garage. A separate door leads to a passage along one side of the house, which connects the series of rooms and patios.

The indoor and outdoor areas are brought together by great glass doors, which slide open to create one vast, single space, backed by a wall of dense vegetation to the rear.

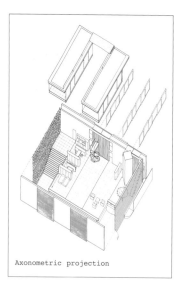

Axonometric projection

Architect: Shigeru Ban

Location: Nishinomiya, Japan

Photography: Hiroyuki Hirai

Although the influence of traditional Japanese architecture can be seen
in this house —
in the fluid
interpretation of
space, the austere
materials, and the
way it relates to
nature — it is also
an imaginative response
to the demands of
modern life.

The three courtyards
are protected from the
weather by awnings that can simply be unfurled.

House H | Sauerbruch & Hutton

This project involved remodeling a three-story Kensington house, built in 1967 by the architect James Melvin. The design is based on a concrete cube measuring 33 x 33 feet (10 x 10 meters) and on a novel concept of space, which combines the original structure with brightly colored new units. Each floor has a different ambience.

On the ground floor a large pane of translucent glass separates the entrance area from the swimming pool and the leafy garden behind it. Here, the interior is separated from the exterior only by sliding glass doors. The first floor is an open space with wide windows on two sides, offering beautiful panoramic views. On the top floor the bedrooms and guest suite are in a private, sensual, and luxurious world of their own.

To keep the space free, appliances and utensils are kept in different brightly colored units on each floor. The contrast between the vivid colors of these shapes and the ever-present garden creates a dense, urban mixture of nature and architecture.

The architects paid great attention to detail. The woodwork, the joins between different materials, and the matching of furniture with walls have all been carefully thought out.

Architects: Sauerbruch & Hutton
Location: London, United Kingdom
Photography: Hélène Binet

First floor

Second floor

Ground floor

The freestanding stairway is like a sculpture rising through the central
section of the building,
its spiraling shape
in contrast with the
right angles that
dominate the spaces
all around it.

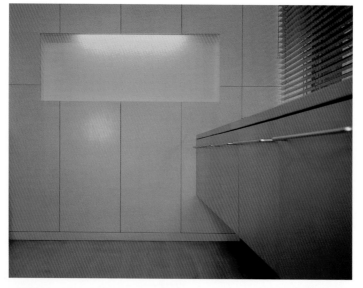

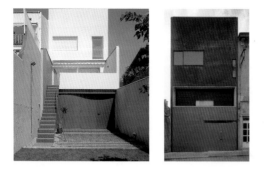

Iborra House | Xavier Llobet/Xavier Ballarín

This is a family home squeezed between party walls in the city of Tarrasa, near Barcelona. On a site measuring only 20 feet (6 meters) wide and some 100 feet (30 meters) from front to back, the architects had little choice but to build the house right up to the edge of the street. This means that, while its private facade faces the garden, its public one is at the full extent of the site.

The house is on four floors. On the ground floor are the entrance and a parking space. A narrow stairway leads up to a hall, which leads in turn to the kitchen, living room, and dining room, looking out onto a large terrace. The wall of the interior staircase, covering two floors in one flight, is paneled in dark red wood so that it stands out clearly on each floor. On the third floor is the main bedroom, with a child's bedroom at the rear. Another staircase leads to the top floor, where a large playroom with a terrace overlooks the garden.

Interestingly, different materials and various sizes of window have been used on the facade, to distinguish each floor from the outside. A slight outward incline on the top floor allows light to enter the playroom at an angle, and a gentle curve in the roof creates unusual reflections.

Architects: Xavier Llobet/Xavier Ballarín
Location: Tarrasa, Barcelona, Spain
Photography: David Cardelús

Fausto Santini in Düsseldorf | Antonio Citterio & Partners

The Fausto Santini boutique in Düsseldorf is part of a global chain that includes three other branches in Paris, Rome, and Milan.

The central idea of this design was to dehumanize the space, stripping it of any accessories to turn it into an abstract icon for a commercial operation, that could be transferred to any capital in the world. It was important to identify the shop with the brand and the goods on sale.

The concept of these four shops is similar to that of an art gallery or museum: formal and classical, neutral and rational, giving pride of place to the objects on display. The flexibility and, oddly enough, the coherence of the global image of these shops has been partly achieved by making good use of the possibilities of each locale – all are on the ground floor of buildings at the commercial heart of each city – and by a uniform choice of materials.

Plaster, stone, and, above all, wood contribute to a sober atmosphere that, apart from a few concessions to a more abstract, modern style, is reminiscent of the 1930s. The idea was to create a neutral space in which the goods themselves provided the only splashes of color.

Architects: Antonio Citterio & Partners
Location: Düsseldorf, Germany
Photography: Gionata Xerra

Antonio Citterio has developed a whole range of tailor-made display methods to show
off the firm's shoes
and bags: a screen
full of holes, glass
shelves with sliding
panels, blocks of
limestone, aluminum
cases and wenge wood
panels. Most of these
have their own lighting.

Giorgio Armani in New York | Peter Marino

Architect Peter Marino's aim here was to create the maximum formal and conceptual tension by using basic geometric structures, limiting the shapes and elements involved, and leaving out any decoration.

The building is a white box, which stands out against a dark background of old brick buildings. It is precisely this dark background, this evidence of the passing of time, which gives it its role as an ideal object, a shiny, abstract container unsullied by the filthy breath of the ephemeral city.

The introversion, withdrawal, and asceticism of this architecture are a reaction to the aggressive chaos of its urban environment. French limestone and glass are used to express this material quality of the building, devoid of social, cultural, or historical content. The structure is of steel on existing foundations. There is no color, only black and white.

The interior is divided into relatively independent spaces, where customers can be given personal attention.

In this building Marino aims for total logic and introduces new concepts of space, scale, perception, and composition, based on a serial, industrial repetition of shapes.

Architect: Peter Marino
Location: New York, USA
Photography: David Cardelús

The simple, symmetrical
facade is based on
a pattern of repeated
squares, which includes
the windows. The rows
of huge windows make
the building look like
one big, highly contemporary display case.

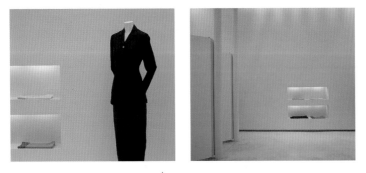

Julie Sohn in Barcelona | Conrado Carrasco and Carlos Tejada

This shop is on the ground floor of a building in the Ensanche area of Barcelona, which is rapidly regaining its former prestige and commercial importance. Typical of the ground-floor locales in this area, it is narrow at the front, stretches a long way back, and has ceilings over 13 feet (4 meters) high.

The basic idea for the design was to create a continuous, neutral space in which garments could be displayed just like the works of art shown in the galleries in this same street. The shop meets the practical requirements of its owners as well as achieving the look they wanted.

The shop is conceived as a tubular container, opening out as you go farther in. The depth of the space and generous height of the ceiling contrast with the minimal show window. The interior was widened by demolishing one of the structural walls. The glass shop front was set slightly back and at an oblique angle to avoid reflections and draw attention to the entrance.

A central, plastered false ceiling conceals lights, loudspeakers, and air-conditioning vents.

Architects: Conrado Carrasco and Carlos Tejada

Location: Barcelona, Spain

Photography: Eugeni Pons

The ceilings and interior partitions are covered in a double layer of
plasterboard to
guard against damp
and structural
shifts. The other
material used in
this design is
matt stainless
steel, in handles,
hangers, and skirting.

Jigsaw in London | John Pawson

Jigsaw had already shown an interest in forceful and original architecture in the design of its previous shops. The starting point for this new one in Bond Street – one of London's smartest shopping streets – was to design a space where the clothes could be shown off in all their glory and where customers would feel comfortable. It was to be a distinctive space that would serve as the flagship store for the company.

Since the facade of the two adjoining buildings that formed the shop had been extensively altered, it was decided to dismantle it and start again from scratch. The new design placed two windows between panels of exquisitely finished concrete. Inside, the first floor is set back from the facade to leave a brightly lit space two stories high, which acts as a show window.

The original floor plan was altered to provide clarity and order. The rectangular geometry is interrupted only by the staircase, which stands out clearly to indicate the presence of another floor. Acrylic screens act as partitions between different areas, creating a secluded atmosphere and reducing the impact of the structural pillars. Wall washers provide general lighting, while spotlights on tracks highlight particular areas.

Architect: John Pawson

Location: London, United Kingdom

Photography: Richard Glover

The whiteness of the walls and superb finish of the granite floor convey
luxury and
sophistication
without being
ostentatious.
Functional
requirements
have been met
expressively,
and with an eye
to proportion.

Giorgio Armani in Paris | Claudio Silvestrin Architects

Claudio Silvestrin's design for the Giorgio Armani shop in Paris echoes the spirit of the 19th-century monasteries also situated here, in the Place Vendôme.

The shop, already occupied by Armani, is on two floors, with show windows facing the square. The firm gave Silvestrin carte blanche for its refurbishment. He rebuilt the stone facade, cleared the rooms, and opened up a series of arches, which later had to be adapted to accommodate modern windows.

For the interior he reverted to a traditional design, creating twin rectangular spaces linked by a staircase and strategically separated by pieces of furniture. Customers using the changing rooms are shielded from public view by walls to the rear of each floor. The main entrance is formed by a stone wall 23 feet (7 meters) high.

Silvestrin is known for the extreme simplicity and monumental character of his interiors and the high quality of his finishes. In this new design he has further refined his purist sensibility, eliminating anything inessential and matching the tones of the interior to the light.

The walls and floors are of stone, whose shade varies according to the amount of natural light falling on them.

Architects: Claudio Silvestrin Architects

Location: Paris, France

Photography: Claudio Silvestrin Architects

The few pieces of furniture consist of high-backed chairs, benches, and tables in African ebony. The whole
space is simple,
harmonious, and
well-proportioned.

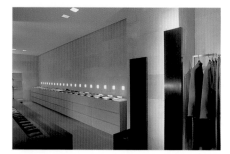

Principe Boutique | Antonio Citterio & Partners

As can be seen in the design of other shops, the similarity between a boutique and an art gallery is no accident. The visitor is invited to wander around a space where a personal view of elegance and luxury is expressed. Bags and accessories, perfectly presented and lit, are displayed not only for sale, but because their very presence and the way they are placed creates an atmosphere, a set of values that the designers are trying to convey. By buying a pair of shoes, the customer buys into this vision of perfection.

The architecture, the materials used for the finishes, the lighting, the furniture, and the products themselves all combine to create a calm, harmonious setting through which the visitor can amble, unhurried and unhindered.

The Principe boutique, in a smart part of central Milan, is a good example of these principles in practice. The limited space available obliged the architects to eliminate all unnecessary elements and put emphasis on the remaining ones. Few materials were used: the entire shop is fitted out using glass, steel, wood, and white-painted plaster. The floor is of marble and the shop front is partly in clear, partly in translucent glass.

Architects: Antonio Citterio & Partners
Location: Milan, Italy
Photography: Gionata Xerra

The display cases
have been designed
with care, in a
combination of wood,
stainless steel, and
glass. They are
independent units
of three different
heights, allowing
flexibility. A false
ceiling, with openings for the lights, conceals the service systems, lighting, and air conditioning.

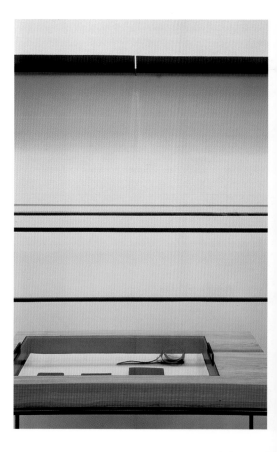

Fendi in Rome | Claudio Lazzarini & Carl Pickering

There is less and less difference today between designer boutiques and art galleries, and the similarities are deliberate. The idea is to give fashion an added cachet and turn the clothes and accessories into something more than objects to be worn. What better way is there to achieve this than to give the sales space a makeover in a simple yet striking modern style, so that the customer or passerby is attracted as much by the shop as by its contents? A great deal of effort is put into drawing people into these shops. Once in, you never know...

This is why the big firms are increasingly putting the design and construction of their international sales points into professional architectural hands. In this case, Fendi entrusted the design of its new shop in Rome to young Italian architects Lazzarini & Pickering, who already enjoy a worldwide reputation for the residential work they have done in recent years. This commercial project was new territory for Lazzarini & Pickering, but they carried it off in their own individual style.

Architects: Claudio Lazzarini & Carl Pickering

Location: Rome, Italy

Photography: Matteo Piazza

Claudio Lazzarini & Carl Pickering have applied their own particular style to this shop, with abundant natural light playing on the color of the interiors; suspended objects that create a sense of lightness; multifunctional, mobile furniture; shiny surfaces; straight lines; symmetrical shapes; and a uniform color scheme.

Louis Vuitton in Paris | Peter Marino & Associates

This design for the Louis Vuitton shop in Paris was commissioned for the launch of a new range of casual wear, to complement its classic collections of suitcases and accessories.

The shop is in an emblematic 1930s art deco building on a corner of the Champs Elysées. A new shop front was designed in glass and bronze, beckoning the visitor into a tall rotunda finished in wood and polished plaster. From here various different routes flow through the store. Aiming for luxury without ostentation, Peter Marino designed the shop along simple, sophisticated lines, to show off the merchandise to best effect.

A glass atrium with exotic wood marquetry provides a visual link between the ground floor and the one below, where another rotunda continues the effect of the entrance.

The men's clothing department has a separate entrance. It has been given a similar look, in perfectly finished, polished plaster. A bronze staircase and glass elevator link the two levels.

Architects: Peter Marino & Associates
Location: Paris, France
Photography: David Cardelús

Woolen carpets on wood floors add warmth
to the show areas.

The simple design
of the shop helps
products stand out clearly and be easily identifiable.

Bottega Veneta | François de Menil

François de Menil's design for Bottega Veneta concentrates on geometry, color, and space, and attempts to take meaningful aesthetic experience to the limits of meaninglessness and obviousness. This is an architectural style that dares to approach absolute formlessness, whose impact lies in the purely physical aspects of mass and material. These may be marked by a slight quiver, some tiny detail, or a casual distortion or fault line in the geometry.

De Menil employs a double strategy in organizing the merchandise on display. Leather goods appear in cases like jewels, idealized objects set in alcoves in the walls, points where all color is concentrated and all attention focused. But they are also used as part of the fabric of the shop as wood or glass might be: as texture, as ingredients in the architecture.

This means that the shopping experience involves the customer in increasingly close contact with the merchandise, from contemplating an item as an idealized object in a display case to appreciating its texture, design, and craftsmanship at close quarters on one of the mobile stands.

Architect: François de Menil
Location: New York, USA
Photography: David Cardelús

The shop, arranged around a showcase wall in the shape of a J, faces the main thoroughfare.

Antonio Pernas in Barcelona | Iago Seara

The shop refurbished by Iago Seara is used to sell a very specific product: Antonio Pernas women's wear. The idea was not only to make the space serve its purpose, but also to identify it immediately with the merchandise on display and the kind of woman for whom it is intended.

The shop has to act as a logo for its contents, representing the brand in its particular market. It has been refurbished using the textures and finishes of natural materials such as wood and stone. For this product and this client group, the style had to reflect the best in contemporary architecture.

The shop is arranged on four levels, two in the basement and two on the ground floor. An existing two-story atrium provides a visual link between all parts of the shop. So as not to obscure this, the stairs were left freestanding on one side. The original facade has been preserved, with additional woodwork. The floors of the interior are in Alicante stone, and the partitions are covered in plasterboard.

Architect: Iago Seara
Location: Barcelona, Spain
Photography: Eugeni Pons

As in other Antonio Pernas shops, because lighting plays a central role in shaping the space, it had to be handled sensitively here. It is used to highlight, emphasize, or add a subtle extra touch to the items on sale, while also creating a pleasant atmosphere in which to shop.

Dr. Baeltz | Shigeru Uchida

This small establishment is rectangular in shape and in three sections, comprising a shop, a customer service counter, and a beauty salon at the rear. The counter is the only element that intrudes into the empty space. All the merchandise is displayed around the walls, and the beauty salon is screened off from the rest of the shop by a panel that does not reach the ceiling and so does not interrupt the continuity of the space.

All Dr. Baeltz products come in simple bottles and packages, arranged on shelves in the side walls. These shelves take the form of a long, narrow display case running behind the counter on one side, and on the opposite side a grid of square box-shelves filling the entire height of the wall.

The finishes on walls and ceiling, the floor of polished marble, the corrugated wood panel holding the display window, and the shiny resin surface of the counter all contribute to the uniform tone of the whole. This is highlighted by overhead illumination from spotlights built into the false ceiling.

Architect: Shigeru Uchida

Location: Tokyo, Japan

Photography: Nacása & Partners

The horizontal
display case
cut into the
wall behind the
customer service
counter is
illuminated from
within. The counter is on two levels and positioned lengthwise along the shop.

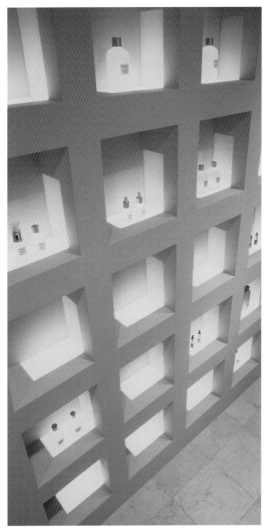

Calvin Klein in New York | John Pawson

Calvin Klein brings together all aspects of his design work under one roof. This shop sells not only men's and women's clothing, bags, and accessories, but also perfume, jewelry, china, and bedroom and bathroom merchandise.

The aim here was to create a space that would express the ideas and vision behind Calvin Klein fashion as well as selling its products.

"In New York, space and light are luxuries," says the American designer. He has realized that, in today's bustling and stressful cities, to be able to enter a calm, ordered place, where everything is immaculate and perfectly arranged, is not only a change of scene but a way into another, more luxurious world.

The shop is on the first four floors of a building with classical facades, previously occupied by the J.P. Morgan bank. The only change made to the exterior was to replace the windows with fixed panes of glass that cover the openings completely, without any wooden frame.

The shop has a total area of 20,000 square feet (1,860 square meters), with ceilings up to 20 feet (6 meters) high.

Architect: John Pawson

Location: New York, USA

Photography: Kristoph Kicherer, David Cardelús

The interior features stone paving, white walls, and, above all, objects placed with great care. No attempt is made, as it is in most shops, to guide the customer's steps in any particular direction. On the contrary, visitors are encouraged to wander at their leisure and soak up the privileged atmosphere. The orderliness of the establishment helps them find their way around.

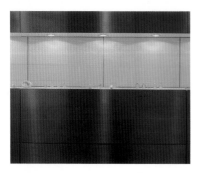

Jeweler's in Munich | Landau & Kindelbacher

Minimalism does not consist only in denial, subtraction, or puritanism. It can also be seen as reducing architecture to its basic elements of space, light, and mass. It is not just a case of eliminating ornament, however, but of celebrating form and space. A good example of the trend can be seen in this design by Landau & Kindelbacher, in which apparently simple architecture masks a highly complex project.

The jeweler's establishment is in a post-war building, in a commercial district of the city. It includes both a sales and display area and a workshop, where jewelry is designed and made for various collections. The shop has a high ceiling and acts as a neutral backdrop for the goods on show.

It was decided not to divide the space in the traditional manner. The partition separating the workshop from the shop was opened up to give a complete view. Transparent display cases and gray walls and flooring emphasize the depth of the space.

The lighting was designed with care, to highlight the pieces on display while remaining unnoticed. Although there are also a few spotlights in the ceiling, the jewels are lit by halogen lamps inside the units.

Architects: Landau & Kindelbacher
Location: Munich, Germany
Photography: Michael Heinrich

The design includes several different showcases. The largest is a block of stainless steel with a band of glass down the middle, where the jewelry is displayed. A counter on wheels, holding the cash register and some drawers, can be pulled out from this. There is also a unit made of maple that revolves around a steel pole. In the show windows, steel-rimmed glass cabinets show off the jewelry without obstructing the view of the shop from outside.

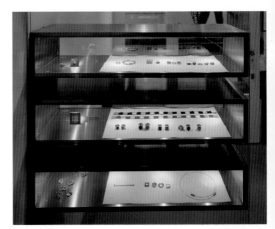

Bulthaup Showroom in Barcelona | Arturo Frediani

This showroom for furniture, kitchens, and household goods occupies the ground floor and basement of a residential building designed by the well-known Catalan architect José Antonio Coderch.

The layout of the homes on the upper floors determines the position of the building's structural walls, an important factor both in dividing up the interior and in linking the ground floor to the level below. A multitude of small decisions, taken over 40 years, had led to alterations that gradually deprived the place of its natural light, sense of space, and flexibility. The architect removed all these additions to clarify and lay bare its complicated geometry.

He has succeeded in rescuing the space, so that what had been a series of closed-up rooms has become a working showroom that follows an intuitive sequence.

The stairs down to the basement were rebuilt and widened. The chunky wooden steps are supported between a wall and a stringboard. Where the wall ends the steps hang, taut, from the strings. In the basement the partitions have disappeared, and daylight comes flooding in for the first time in 40 years. A large, single-paned, hinged window opens onto the inner courtyard.

Architect: Arturo Frediani

Location: Barcelona, Spain

Photography: Eugeni Pons

The practical side of things has been dealt
with using a
minimum of rough
and ready elements.
L-shaped metal
skirting beads
mask the joins
between walls
and floors.

Elevation Salon + Café | Petersen & Verwers

This large hairdressing salon is in a business district of San Francisco. The client had asked for the maximum use to be made of the working space and for a timeless, elegant, and sophisticated atmosphere. In this design a café provides the focal point of the interior, which is a long space beginning with a narrow shop front on the street and opening out toward the back.

The cylindrical form of the café, contrasting with the rigid framework around it, is conceived as the centerpiece, a meeting point between stylists and clients. It also gives this large space a more intimate feel and creates a swirl of movement through the salon.

Architectural elements were carefully placed to emphasize the feeling of spaciousness. The administrative and service areas are concentrated along one side, to leave the rest of the space free. The partitions of these areas do not reach the ceiling, so that the whole place is a single unit.

Lighting plays an important part in creating the atmosphere. Indirect lighting increases the sense of height and is complemented by soft light sources above the mirrors in the workspaces, and halogen lamps in the ceiling.

Architects: Petersen & Verwers
Location: San Francisco, USA
Photography: Todd Verwers

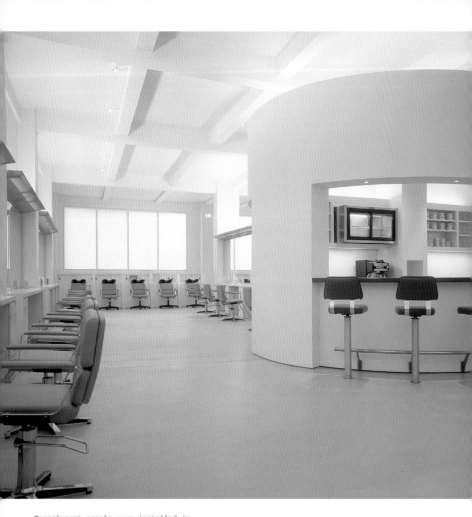

Translucent panels were installed in
the rear windows
to shut out the
view of the alley
and bathe the
space in diffuse
natural light.

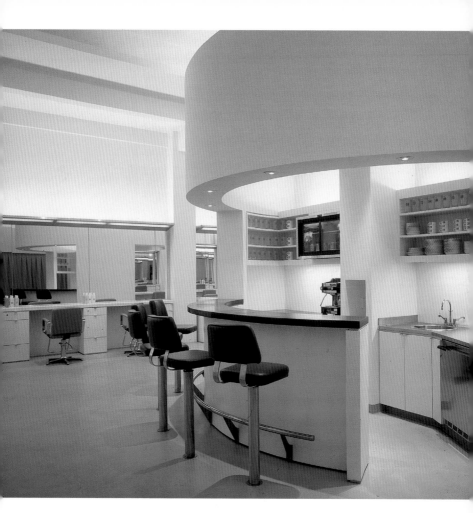

The reception
desk, stylists'
workstations,
washing area, and
lights were all
designed to match
the client's
taste and practical requirements.

Hotel Ace | Eric Hentz/Mallet

This hotel was previously an old boarding house in the Belltown district of Seattle, an area that has been changing for some time now, with new restaurants opening and a massive increase in the number of apartment buildings.

The client wanted a hotel in the style of New York's SoHo: modern and eye-catching. Despite a limited budget, great results were achieved thanks to the architects' imaginative choice of materials and finishes. The success of the hotel's image is largely due to the handling of light and volume, on a site with little of either.

The entrance to the hotel is through a glass door and a vestibule, from which a steep, narrow wooden staircase can just be discerned. Upstairs there is a stone reception area, with a lobby to the left. Although this room is not large, the combined effect of the shiny white panels on some of the walls, the walnut flooring, and large skylight creates the impression of a much larger space, something unexpected given the narrow stairway.

Architects: Eric Hentz/Mallet

Location: Seattle, USA

Photography: Jim Henkers, Chad Brown

In some of the bedrooms, the bathroom
door forms part
of the wall when
shut. In others,
the doors consist
of white glass
panels suspended
from anodized
aluminum poles.

Nil Bar and Restaurant | Claudio Lazzarini & Carl Pickering

The concept behind this bar and restaurant is that of a blank page inscribed with graphics and space. The design is made up of three architectural elements: a runway that also serves as a long bench, a system of white curtains that open and close off certain spaces and perspectives, and a bar formed by a block of light with a screen. Restaurants are theatrical places, and the drama of Nil lies in its great capacity for transformation.

The runway is like a stage: anyone who walks along it can see and be seen by everyone else. After dinner, it becomes a place to sit and relax, or may even become a dance floor.

The restaurant can be transformed at any time in various ways, through the use of electronically operated curtains. When drawn, they create two oval spaces, one around the bar and the other around a more private dining area at the back of the restaurant.

The computer-controlled halogen lighting changes constantly, and makes the whole place throb. Video equipment varies the ambient color and projects moving images.

Architects: Claudio Lazzarini & Carl Pickering
Location: Rome, Italy
Photography: Hiroshi Ueda

Several arts videos
have been shown here,
including shorts by
Paolo Canevari and
Adrian Tranquilli.
The large marble
slabs are for
sitting, singing, or dancing on.

The most interesting feature of this restaurant is not that it is all white, but its capacity for physical, musical, and visual transformation. It can change completely from one moment to the next. This is a recurring theme in the work of some designers.

Casa Pilar Café-Bar | A-cero Architects

A large bar runs the length of the Casa Pilar, while other, smaller, bar-shaped tables are sited near the entrance. These appear to float in the air, and create an informal atmosphere ideal for snacks. The kitchen, at the far end of the bar, communicates directly with a dining area to the rear of the space. Here there are big, long tables at which to relax and enjoy a good meal. The bathrooms are in the middle, where they are easily accessible from all areas.

The whole space is drenched in white light, which comes in through the main facade and from the yard at the back of the building. This natural light is reinforced in the interior by lights tucked around the edges of the false ceiling, which also conceals the air-conditioning and other service systems.

The floors are in reddish merbau wood and the furniture is minimal. The bar-tables are simple, L-shaped pieces of beech, and the tables, also in beech, are very plain. Black and white "Ant" chairs by Arne Jacobsen were chosen to complement this clean, pure ambience. All the walls and ceilings are white, and a sheet of opaque glass hangs from a rail to give privacy to one table set apart from the rest.

Architects: A-cero Architects
Location: La Coruña, Spain
Photography: Juan Rodríguez

The facade is set back, leaving room for two bar-tables outside, next to the entrance. This is a nice touch that communicates what goes on inside without the need for garish signs.

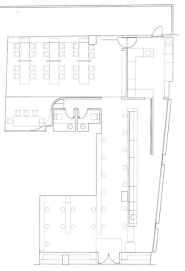

Floor plan

Nodo Restaurant | Dani Freixes/Varis Architects

This restaurant was originally a bank on two floors, with unframed square windows and stone-clad floors, a few walls, and the staircase. It was decided to keep the existing décor, complementing it with a paneled beechwood ceiling in three colors, divided into different-sized squares with gaps between them. This is used to disguise technical installations. The same paneling in a similar pattern is used on the walls, providing continuity and contrasting warmly with the stone flooring.

Several glass screens, lined with thin sheets of wood and lit from behind by fluorescent lamps, are positioned so as to provide direct lighting for the tables and bar.

All the furniture on the ground floor, including the bar and a long bench, is in beech, stained to match one of the colors in the ceiling. The washbowls in the bathrooms are also set into wooden units, and positioned facing the windows to give views of the garden. The cubicles are in wood and laminated glass, so that they let in natural light by day and at night become lanterns, lit from the inside.

Architects: Dani Freixes/Varis Architects
Location: Madrid, Spain
Photography: Mihail Moldoveanu

An orderly arrangement of lights, fitted into round, domed recesses in the ceiling, provides uniform, indirect illumination. This is complemented by lantern-screens of wood and laminated glass, which allow the room to be organized in different ways.

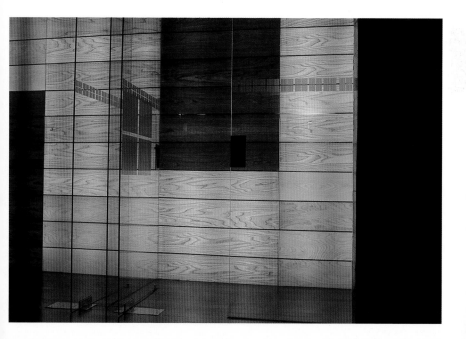

One Happy Cloud Restaurant | Claesson Koivisto Rune Arkitektkontor

A preoccupation with light and simplicity in interior design, traditional in Japan, is also common in Scandinavian architecture.

The manager of the One Happy Cloud Japanese restaurant in Stockholm did not wish simply to turn his establishment into a picturesque sushi bar, but wanted a fusion of Japanese and Scandinavian style and cuisine.

The result is a place of extraordinary elegance and simplicity, with no direct references to Japanese culture, but many subtle allusions to the peaceful atmosphere of that country's traditional architecture.

The total floor plan is roughly square, with an area of about 1,600 square feet (150 square meters). The restaurant itself is organized as two narrow rooms in the form of an L, and the kitchen and utility areas take up the rest of the space. The tables are arranged in a line along the outer walls.

High ceilings, diffuse light coming through translucent screens, simple, chunky furniture, and an absence of architectural detail combine to create an impression of restraint, distinctive yet unpretentious.

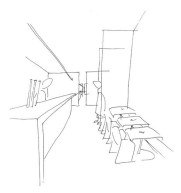

Architects: Claesson Koivisto Rune
Arkitektkontor
Location: Stockholm, Sweden
Photography: Patrick Engquist

Existing walls and frosted glass partitions are used to divide the space into smaller, more intimate
rooms. All the walls
are plastered and
painted white, except
for a wall at one end
and another behind
the bar, which are
covered in drawings
by graphic artist
Nill Svensson on
a black background.

Isometric drawing

El Japonés Restaurant | López/Tarruella

The design of this restaurant is a reinterpretation of Japanese style. On either side of the entrance, tall bamboo canes are placed to make a statement.

The use of straight, powerful, austere shapes; the combination of warm and cold materials; and the contrasts in color and texture, matt and shiny surfaces, are all echoes of Japanese style. In the bathrooms, the red interiors are reminiscent of Japanese lacquer and contrast with the zinc sheets used for the exteriors of the cubicles and for the kitchen.

A large wall some 80 feet (24 meters) long has been covered in padding overlaid with metal gauze, to solve problems with acoustics.

There are seating options for individuals, at the bar; for couples, at small tables next to the soundproof walls; and for groups. The polished slabs of wood used for the floors, the long benches, the bar tops, and the shared tables help create the desired atmosphere of informality, openness, and flexibility.

Chairs and stools are the only other furniture. The Hans Wegner chairs and the Jamaica stools by Pepe Cortés fit in well with the wooden tables without being swallowed up by the whole.

Architects: López/Tarruella
Location: Barcelona, Spain
Photography: Eugeni Pons

Suspended over the two large tables at the front is a
pair of lamps by
Ingo Maurer. Hanging
from these are little
pieces of paper with
notes scribbled on
them, like offerings
at a Buddhist shrine.

Wagamama Restaurant | David Chipperfield Architects

Wagamama, a Japanese restaurant in London's Soho, occupies the ground floor and basement of a building with a broad facade but not much depth.

The dining area is in the basement while the kitchen is on the ground floor. David Chipperfield has given much thought to the customers' route from street to table. In the facade, seven floor-to-ceiling openings paneled in glass ensure that the restaurant is visible from the street. The eighth opening is the entrance.

The ground floor is slightly above street level. Once inside, customers wait to be led to their tables in a long corridor from which they can watch dishes being prepared in the kitchen. A screen of frosted glass separates them from the street and the drop down to the basement. At night their silhouettes can be seen from outside against the glass.

Downstairs, wooden tables and benches are arranged at right angles to the passageway and the well beyond it. Dishes are sent down from the kitchen via dumbwaiters in anodized aluminum, from where they are taken to the tables.

Architects: David Chipperfield Architects
Location: London, United Kingdom
Photography: Richard Davies

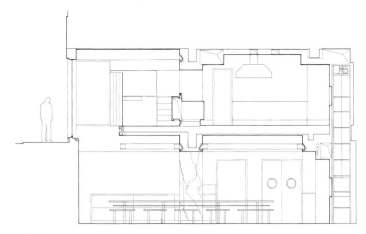

Cross section

The entrance steps, the main stairs, and both floors are tiled in warm gray. All the walls are tiled in white, except the main basement wall, which is paneled in oak. The two large pillars in the middle of the dining area are faced with red marble.

No Picnic Office | Claesson Koivisto Rune Arkitektkontor

No Picnic is a Swedish industrial design company whose head office is in a 1930s factory building. When commissioned to give this building a completely new design, the architects felt it was important, given the creative nature of the company, to turn it into a dynamic, open space.

Private areas were also required so that projects could be handled with discretion. The architects' solution was to split the space vertically on three levels. The basement houses the technical department; the reception floor has the entrance and common areas such as the kitchen, meeting rooms, and workshop; and a more private upper level contains the design room.

Though the layout is quite clear, the architects describe their design as labyrinthine because of the way the staircase divides up the space. Running through the middle of the building, between two walls parallel to the main facade, it grows narrower as it ascends. It has a great visual impact, reminiscent of Dutch neoplasticism. Its walls vary in height according to the requirements of the offices bordering it.

Architects: Claesson Koivisto Rune Arkitektkontor

Location: Stockholm, Sweden

Photography: Patrik Engquist

The maquette workshop is on the upper floor and is two stories high. It is a bright, open space that calls to mind its industrial past.

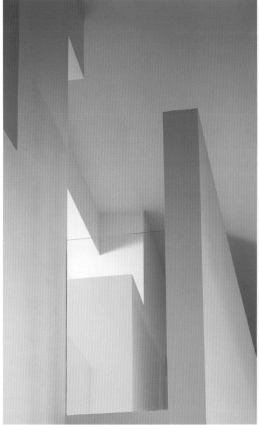

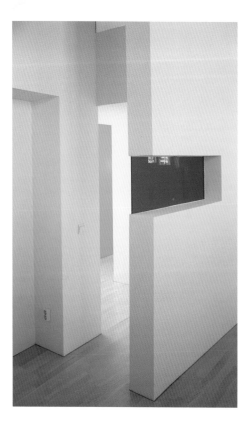

The choice of
materials softens
the strict, formal
lines of the design.
The plastered walls,
the brick facade,
and the false ceilings
are painted white.
The handling of light
is especially striking:
great care has been
taken to ensure that
daylight reaches the whole space.

Office of Rifé i Associats | Francesc Rifé

This interior-design studio is located on one of Barcelona's main thoroughfares, on the ground floor of a residential and office building. It is on two floors: the entrance, leading to a small lobby and a showcase, is at street level, while the workspaces are on the lower ground floor.

You enter through a low doorway, behind which the small lobby faces a glass door and a glazed cabinet in which various design items are displayed. This exhibition is changed from time to time.

Behind the door, a freestanding metal staircase leads down to the hall. Its curved banister contrasts with its rigid structure. The work area is divided in two. Opposite the showcase, in full view of passersby, there is a table at which two or three designers can work. Next door, away from public view, is a room with a desk and computers for administrative work, a general space with a portable table for meetings, and another private workspace.

A long unit of built-in drawers disguises irregularities in the wall. Three wooden units to the rear hold the filing system and a bathroom.

Architect: Francesc Rifé
Location: Barcelona, Spain
Photography: Joan Mundó

There is nothing ordinary about this clean-cut space, where the few pieces of furniture hardly touch the maple-wood floor. The meeting table is multipurpose and easily portable.

The low
front door
is of glass
surrounded
by gray
stone. The
wall inside
the showcase
is of the
same stone.
This entrance
prepares you
for the plunge
into the bright,
open space glimpsed from the street.

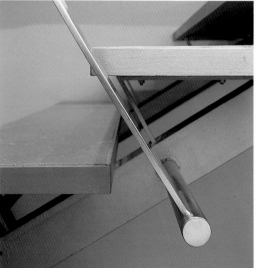

Recoletos Publishing House | Wortmann Bañares Architects

The head office of Recoletos publishers in Barcelona is in a modern office block, with curtain-wall facades, impeccably finished surfaces, widely spaced pillars some 20 to 30 feet (7 to 10 meters) apart, an almost perfectly symmetrical floor plan, raised floors to house service systems, and false ceilings. The building already met many needs and had established a strong precedent from which it was hard to deviate. It seemed that the only thing left to do was to choose from the wide selection of screens and office furniture available.

Guillermo Bañares and Johannes Wortmann have succeeded in combating the hierarchical symmetry, compact image, and technological pragmatism of the building with alternative strategies and interpretations that, without discarding what was already there, enrich a working environment that would otherwise be excessively uniform.

Rather than using screens to form compartments, Bañares and Wortmann created a more fluid space in which different work areas are separated by shelves and cupboards. They used different degrees of transparency and provided more interesting routes through the space. They also introduced unusual materials such as fiber-cement, and chose furniture that would age with time.

Architects: Wortmann Bañares Architects
Location: Barcelona, Spain
Photography: Joan Mundó

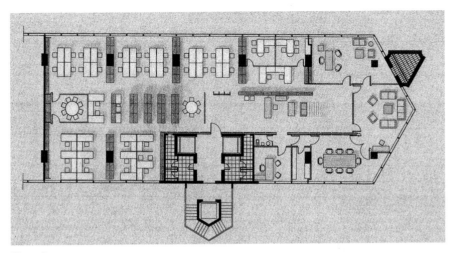

Floor plan

Any jarring elements in this design, such as the overly uniform plasterboard false ceiling, are, paradoxically, due to the fact that the original building was too polished.

Osho International Offices | Daniel Rowen

This design was for the New York headquarters of an international publishing house specializing in Zen philosophy and meditation. The aim was to create an ambience that reflected the concept behind the firm and the lifestyle of the people who work there.

The offices occupy the 46th floor of a well-known skyscraper on New York's Lexington Avenue. This tall, slim tower has an unusually small floor area, measuring about 3,000 square feet (285 square meters), with a central nucleus of installations and an elevator shaft on the south side.

One priority was to combine the lobby, reception, and conference room in a single space. This central common area is bordered on two facing sides by storage cabinets stretching from floor to ceiling. These also contain the infrastructure of the communications system. On the side opposite the elevators, a screen of translucent frosted glass closes off other, smaller, more private rooms.

From the entrance, one catches glimpses of the shadowy movements of people behind this glass screen.

Architect: Daniel Rowen
Location: New York, USA
Photography: Michael Moran

Seen from the corridor, the glass screen reflects the activities going on around it, and emphasizes the more private nature of the individual offices.

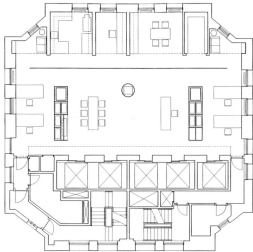

Finance Office | Wortmann Bañares Architects

This office space of 4,300 square feet (400 square meters) houses the headquarters of a finance company controlling the electronic flow of vast sums of money, whose only physical presence is a flicker of figures on a screen.

Unlike many other contemporary designers, who attempt to imitate cyberspace, Bañares and Wortmann give virtual reality its place as an object of contemplation, but do not allow it to determine the overall design.

Their idea is to incorporate information technology in the workplace in subtle ways. Though it is true that new technology has changed our perception of reality, our feelings for certain kinds of space, furniture, and materials have not changed in the same way. Bañares and Wortmann do not think it appropriate to reproduce a cyber-look in their architecture, preferring to hint at it more indirectly.

They have responded to the screens, with their flickering images, by including polished surfaces and translucent glass, which create reflections and transparencies as an extension of the traditional office.

Architects: Wortmann Bañares Architects

Location: Barcelona, Spain

Photography: Lluís Casals

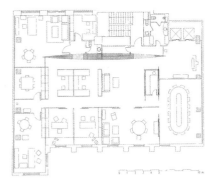

Floor plan

Despite the major part played by information technology in the firm's work, its offices still have a surprisingly calm and domestic appearance. The design does not fall into the trap of virtual reality, but goes back to more important principles: ease of use and making sure that the people who work there feel comfortable about the space.

Office of GCA Architects | GCA Architects

This office is part of the ordinary urban landscape of Barcelona, occupying a former textile warehouse on the ground floor of a building dating from 1946.

There were already some classically designed offices near the main entrance, with moldings and compartments, while the rest of the space was open plan.

It was decided to adopt a double strategy: to preserve the look of the existing areas at the front, restoring the woodwork and installing service systems so that they could be used for reception, administration, and management; and to counterbalance this by creating a totally modern space in the warehouse, to be used for architectural design.

The plan is based on a dialog of opposites. In the end, however, it is the design area that dominates the whole office. It is conceived as a vast, white box, illuminated from above by two large skylights, in which the various different areas – design and drawings room, project management room – follow the order of the work to be done on a given project. This sequence ends in a large outdoor patio.

Architects: GCA Architects
Location: Barcelona, Spain
Photography: Jordi Miralles

Faculty of Law | Aranda, Pigem, and Vilalta

This Faculty of Law is on the Montilivi campus on the outskirts of Gerona. The building features the key characteristics favored by these architects (who are based in the small town of Olot). It combines powerful bulk, plenty of varied exterior space, perfect control of natural light, an ability to emphasize or disguise certain aspects of the building, and meticulous attention to the details of construction.

The building is a mixture of solid masses and empty expanses. There are two kinds of empty space: exterior spaces such as patios and terraces; and interior spaces, including atriums, walkways, and passages. They are enriched by the solidity around them: the sensual finishes, the range of textures in the materials used, and the varied play of light upon them. The structure itself is visually of secondary importance.

Since the functional layout of the interior is complex, it is not reflected in the facades. The building is entirely encased in a material that allows natural light to enter evenly, unifying the whole. Only the vertical slits illuminating the inner courtyards interrupt this uniform exterior.

Architects: Aranda, Pigem, and Vilalta

Location: Gerona, Spain

Photography: Eugeni Pons

The architects had to come up with a way to deal with the pronounced slope
of the site. To
preserve its sense
of autonomy, the
building rises
from the ground
on a strong, solid
projecting foundation (socle).

The Faculty of Law is the result of an elaborate creative process, based on a consideration of the location and its surroundings as well as very specific functional requirements. The success of the design lies in having produced a building that is both practical and a delight to the senses.

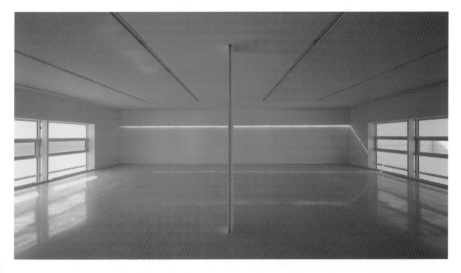

Primary School in Vienna | Götz/Manahl

This site, on the outskirts of the city, is on a busy street in a mixed urban environment. It has been almost entirely built up, leaving only four open spaces: three at the rear looking out onto dense rows of houses, and an inner yard.

The main building is rectangular and faces the sports field. It houses the entrance, bathrooms, and classrooms. A multifunctional hall, gym, and canteen are slotted into the remaining triangular area around the inner open space. To the south there are a library, administrative offices, and staff rooms. At the very end, in an annex on the same side, is the caretaker's apartment.

The upper floors look west, with views over the city through large windows. The three blocks of classrooms, facing west and south, look out over the green open space of the sports field. These rooms can be adapted as necessary to form one or two large classrooms, or several smaller ones, simply by moving the partitions between them.

Architects: Götz/Manahl

Location: Vienna, Austria

Photography: Rupert Steiner

Top floor

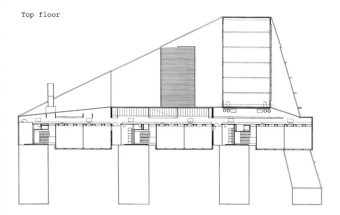

The metal sheets covering the exterior of the building give it a sober, industrial appearance. The interiors are in bare concrete with light-colored floors, the only decoration provided by a few elements painted in basic colors.

New World School | Adolf Krischanitz

This project involved converting and extending a home to turn it into a school. The house is a small building on two stories, built around supporting walls, and the extension block is on one floor. The entrance and stairs are sandwiched between the two blocks.

Without a doubt, the most attractive features of this design are the choice of materials and the treatment of the exterior. The walls have been covered in dark gray mortar. The arrangement of the windows is totally abstract and regular. The original facade had a grid of ten identical vertical rectangles, arranged in two rows, and the new block has been given one long window at ground level.

The windows all have mirrored glass. The building is like a black hole, absorbing all the light coming in from outside and giving back only spectacular reflections. Fragments of landscape stand out against the dark, blind, hermetic walls: distorted trees, the base of a trunk, a branch against the sky, the ghost of a house in the distance.

Architect: Adolf Krischanitz

Location: Schwarzenstockallee, Vienna, Austria

Photography: Margherita Spiluttini

"The theme of this building is unity underlying multiplicity: the interior,
the visible, nature
(art), art (nature),
sameness and
difference, the
chemistry of
perception, the
artist's palette
as a driving force
behind meaning."
(Adolf Krischanitz)

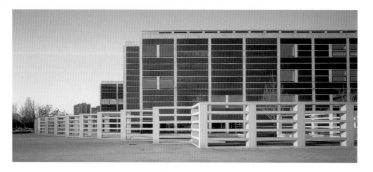

Barcelona Concert Hall | Rafael Moneo

This monolithic, formally laid-out building houses many activities. As well as two concert halls, one seating 2,340, the other 610, it contains all the facilities to go with them: rehearsal rooms for performers and orchestras, a museum of music, a specialist library, the Higher Institute of Music, recording studios, suites for experimental music, restaurants, workshops, and shops.

Located as it is in a sparsely developed area of Barcelona, it is not intended to relate to its surroundings. It consists of a huge box formed by a grid of bare reinforced concrete, the gaps covered with stainless steel plates on the exterior and lined with maple wood on the interior.

The foyer is a public space, like a covered square where cars and pedestrians can mingle, dominated by an enormous lantern skylight. The severe solidity of the exterior encloses this monumental empty space, which is the hub of the whole design and the starting point for all other activities. It provides a clear separation between the two auditoriums, a distinction that is lost on the upper and basement floors where dressing rooms and other facilities serve both halls.

Architect: Rafael Moneo

Location: Barcelona, Spain

Photography: David Cardelús

The vast skylight is suspended over the entrance area,
like a huge container
for this singular space.

Children's Day Nursery | Elsa Prochazka

The use of materials common in Viennese modernism, particularly in the work of Josef Frank and Ernst Lichtblau, lifts this building out of mere elegant asceticism into nobility.

The commission for this day-nursery involved extending a complex of houses made up of rows of blocks on different levels. The new block is at right angles to these, connected to them by a portico. Making use of the slope, the building is raised from the ground to create a covered outdoor space. It has three large rooms and rests on three cubic pillars, which hold the service systems and storage for outdoor equipment.

The concepts are clearly expressed, without recourse to interior decoration. The building is autonomous, faces the desired direction, and has large play areas protected from the weather. The platform running along its eastern side provides a visual link between interior and exterior.

The facades are covered in panels of orange-brown glass, which give the building a liquid appearance, as though it were a log reflected in water.

Architect: Elsa Prochazka
Location: Carminweg, Austria
Photography: Rupert Steiner

The architect has made use of the sloping site to create several covered
areas, sheltered
from the weather.
The complex also
has an outdoor
playing field.

Cross section

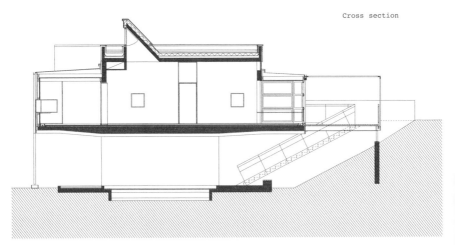

Epilogue

And tomorrow? More out of less

Minimalism has been defined and interpreted in many different ways: as a legacy of Cistercian architecture, the result of modern functionalism, the evolution of various artistic movements of the 1960s, or a lesson in Japanese austerity. Despite all these different visions, however, it has always manifested itself in the same way: as a reduction of architecture to the basic concepts of space, light, and mass.

This tendency to seek simplicity (bearing in mind that art and architecture are intrinsically complex disciplines) has become fashionable. Claudio Silvestrin designs shops for Giorgio Armani, John Pawson's monograph is a best-seller, and loft owners everywhere crave this clean, monochrome style. As ever in the cyclical development of artistic movements, minimalism emerged after the opulence of the 1980s as a soothing response to excess, a bastion of calm against the bombardment of stimuli that is modern life.

...minimalism emerged as a soothing response to excess...

…minimalism has created real luxury…

One of the reasons why minimalism has become a cult is that it has created real luxury. In the old days, cornices were used to cover the join between walls and ceilings, since this was often cracked. Baseboards were provided because the part of the wall next to the floor often got dirty. Nowadays, if you are rich enough, you can leave the merest line of shadow under your walls, as if they were floating, and when they get dirty you can pay someone to repaint them. In any case, it is not just a question of how things look. Clients are enchanted by this precise construction method and the apparently simple finishes it offers.

The architecture of recent years has often been described as anorexic. In this exhaustive book we have amply demonstrated that only the most unthinking observer would confuse minimalist space with empty space, and that this style is a quest for essences, not for nothingness.

Paradoxically, minimalism is both a search for timelessness and a passing fashion. The question is whether it is a serious approach that might become a permanent force in art and architecture, or merely an empty option that in time will be discarded along with Calvin Klein underwear.

It is impossible to tell what the future holds for minimalism, but if past experience of stylistic trends is anything to go by, a change is due very soon. The concepts of austerity, whiteness, subtlety, and sobriety have all been exploited to the full and cannot be taken any further over the next few years without becoming repetitive. There is no scope left for stimulating or revealing contributions here.

Minimalism as a theoretical movement, however, is timeless and will not die. It will adapt to new habits and become a way of

…this style is a quest for essences, not for nothingness…

life, based on an approach that has influenced people's behavior since time immemorial: the attempt to reap the maximum reward from minimum effort.

A magnificent example of this savoir-faire is the Eames house in California. Prefabricated units and cheap construction methods were used to complete the building quickly and on a low budget. The interior of the house, however, is far from minimalist. It is full of carpets, sculptures, family souvenirs, and everything that goes to make a warm, comfortable home. This is a splendid example of minimalist architecture without white walls or continuous paving.

...minimalism as a theoretical movement is timeless and will not die...

...That is how minimalism will survive, making more out of less...

Minimalism should continue as a creative inclination to get the most from the least, not just economically, but also in choosing building materials. Natural resources are running out, and too much energy has been wasted in recent years. Ecological awareness is vital: a small decision may benefit not only a design, but also the entire ecosystem.

Aesthetically, it should still be possible, using existing examples and a little talent, to continue creating sensual spaces in which to dream, spaces stripped of anything superfluous, imbued with a peaceful sense of order. That is how minimalism will survive, making more out of less.